LEBANESE CUISINE

For Amin
For Ruchdi, Tarek and Ziad
For Odette
And in memory of Laurice, who helped me
take my first steps as a cook,
and Massoud, whose legacy to me
was a love of gardens.

Andrée Maalouf

To Audrey, with delectation
For Hugo, Camille and Sara.

Karim Haïdar

ISBN: 978-0-86356-644-8

First published in French as *Cuisine Libanaise D'Hier et D'Aujourd'hui* by Albin Michel, Paris, in 2007

This edition published by Saqi in 2010

Copyright © Éditions Albin Michel, 2007
Copyright © Saqi, 2010
Photography © Caroline Faccioli, 2007, 2010
Translation copyright © Lulu Norman and Sophie Lewis, 2010

A full CIP record for this book is available from the British Library.
A full CIP record for this book is available from the Library of Congress.

Manufactured in Lebanon

SAQI

26 Westbourne Grove, London W2 5RH, UK
2398 Doswell Avenue, Saint Paul, Minnesota, 55108, US
Verdun, Beirut, Lebanon
www.saqibooks.com

Lebanese Cuisine

Past and Present

Andrée Maalouf & Karim Haïdar

Preface by Amin Maalouf

SAQI

Contents

Preface *By Amin Maalouf*   9

Introduction *By Andrée Maalouf & Karim Haïdar*   11

MEZZE: THE IMAGE OF DIVERSITY   13
Lebanese Salads   14
    Fattoush 15
    Tabbouleh 16
    Tomatoes with Cumin 18
    Artichoke Hearts and Broad Bean Salad 18
    Rocket with Olives 19
Vegetables   20
    Stuffed Vine Leaves 21
    Okra with Olive Oil 22
    Green Beans with Olive Oil 22
    Aubergine Maghmour 24
Cooking with Sesame   26
    Moutabal 27
    Courgettes Moutabal 28
    Swiss Chard Moutabal 28
    Tahini-Based Sauces 29
    Tarator Sauce 29
    Tajine Sauce 29
    Hummus 30
Pulses   32
    Moudardara 33
    Yellow Lentil Salad 33
    Moujaddara, A Biblical Dish 34
    Coral Lentil Moujaddara 35
    Falafel 36
    Pickled Turnips 37
Mouajanats   38
    Mana'ish, Round Flat Bread with Zaatar. 39
    Rekakats, Pastry Wraps with Cheese and Parsley 40
    Sambousiks 41
    Lahm Bi Ajeen, Small Lamb and Tomato Tarts 42
    Fatayers with Spinach 44
Lebanese Cheeses   46
    Shanklish in Salad 47
    Fried Halloumi 48

Labneh 49

SOUPS   51

Adas Bi Hamod, Lentil Soup with Swiss Chard and Lemon 52
Coral Lentil Soup with Tomato 54
Yellow Lentil Soup 54
Chicken Soup with Vermicelli 55
Hamiss, Sweet Onion Soup 55
Winter Vegetable Soup 56

KIBBEH   59

Pumpkin Kibbeh 62
Fried Kibbeh Balls 63
Kibbeh Meshwiyeh 64
Kibbeh Nayyeh, Tartare of Kibbeh 65
Fish Kibbeh 66
Kibbeh Bil-Saynieh, Oven-Baked Kibbeh 68
Kibbeh with Yoghurt 69
Khiar Bi Laban, Yoghurt with Cucumber 69

VEGETABLE DISHES   71

Yakhnet-Bemieh, Greek Horn or Okra Ragout 72
Yakhnet-Ardichawkeh, Ragout of Artichoke Hearts 73
Yakhnet-Bazellah, Pea Ragout 74
Yakhnet-Batata, Potato Ragout 76
Yakhnet-Loubieh, Green Bean Ragout 77
Basmati Rice 77
Rice with Vermicelli 77
Yakhnet-Fassouliah, White Bean Ragout 78
Aubergine Fatteh 79
Fattet-Halioun, with Asparagus 80
Fattet-Hummus, with Chickpeas 80
Fattet-Khodra, with Vegetables 82
Aubergines with Ewe's Milk Yoghurt 83
Koussa Bil-Laban, Courgettes Stuffed with Lamb and Yoghurt 84
Ablama, Selection of Stuffed Vegetables 86
Stuffed Cabbage Leaves 88
Sheikh El-Mehshi, Stuffed Aubergines 88
Stuffed Courgettes and Stuffed Vine Leaves 89

MEAT AND POULTRY DISHES   91

Kaftahs   92

Oven-Baked Kaftah 93
Kaftah Nayyeh, Tartare of Kaftah 94

Grilled Kaftah 94
Fried Kaftah Meatballs 95

Grilled Meats   96

Quail with Sumac 97
Lamb Cutlets with 7 Spices 97
Shish Taouk 98
Toum Bezeit, Cream of Garlic with Oil 98
Farrouj Meshwi, Grilled Chicken with Garlic 99

Festive Dishes   100

Leg Of Lamb with Rice and Broad Beans 101
Five Spice Lamb and Rice 102
Freekket-Touyour with Three Birds 104
Bulgur Bedfeen 104
Royal Mouloukhieh 106
Seven Spice Chicken and Rice 107
Maqloubet-Batenjan, Aubergine Layer Cake 108
Lamb and Wheat Hrisseh with Cinnamon 110
Daoud Basha, Minced Lamb Balls 111
Bulgur Wheat with Tomato 111
Masbaht-El-Darwish 112

FISH DISHES   115

Sayadieh 116
Royal Sea Bream with Aubergine 118
Spicy Grey Mullet 118
Octopus Salad with Coriander 119
Squid with Garlic and Coriander 120
Sabbidij, Cuttlefish in Ink 122
The Sultan of Fish, with Deep-Fried Cauliflower and Aubergine. 123
Fish Freekeh 124

SWEETS   127

Haytaliyeh 128
Walnut Marzipan Cake 130
Meghli 131
Atayef-Bil-Ashta 132
Easter Maamoul 134
Awamats, Doughnuts in Syrup 136
Khsheif 137
Snayniyeh 138
Strawberry and Orange-Blossom Salad 140
Pears in Arak 142
Maakaroun 144
Apples and Bananas with Cinnamon 145
Riz-Bi-Halib, Lebanese Rice Pudding 145
Osmallieh 146

ICE CREAM 149

Halva Ice Cream 150
Strawberry Ice Cream 150
Sahlab Ice Cream 151
Rose Ice Cream 151

COFFEE 153

Black Coffee 154
White Coffee 154
Aniseed Kaak 155
Kaak Teta Nazeera 155
Sfouf 156

LEBANESE PRODUCTS 159

Bulgur Wheat 160
Lebanese Breads 161
Sumac 162
Pine Nuts 163
Zaatar 164
Spices 165
The Aleppo Mix or 5 Spice Mix 165
The 7 Spice Mix 165
Debs Remmane, Pomegranate Molasses 166
Carob Molasses 166
Grape Molasses 167
Tahini, Sesame Paste 167
Freekeh 168
Mazahr, Orange-Blossom Water 169
Maward, Rose Water 169

Where to Find Lebanese Products and Spices 170

Acknowledgements 171

Index 172

Preface

Amin Maalouf

For those who have left their country, cookery is – if I dare distort a famous saying – what remains of the original culture when everything else has been forgotten. All migrant peoples know this, particularly the Lebanese, who for decades have spread out into the world, often changing their names, forgetting their language, losing their historical and sociological markers. Only their cuisine has been handed down, from generation to generation. And it has done better than survive; it has been reborn in Paris, London, Rio, Montreal and New York, in Jeddah, Dubai and Jerusalem, supremely indifferent to political borders and areas of civilisation. And so successfully that this tiny, fragile, vulnerable country has become – in one field only, to the exclusion of all others – a respected, conquering, quasi-imperial "power". So modern Lebanese people have in a sense reproduced the exploits of the ancient Phoenicians, a distinctly feminine race who preferred to conquer by cunning rather than warfare, which earned them nothing but continual mockery.

For the daughters and sons of this nation ill-treated by History, such a remarkable expansion is, unsurprisingly, a source of legitimate pride, but it also gives rise to a question: having left its native soil to establish itself on the whole world's tables, can Lebanese cuisine remain itself even as it opens up to the tastes and sensibilities of other peoples? The question is especially valid in that Lebanese cooking tends to the repetitive, indeed the ritualistic. One judges the standard of a new restaurant first by the way it prepares a small number of symbolic dishes, beginning with the irreplaceable hummus – what garnish is used, the particular flavours and texture … Anyone looking to innovate, to shake up habits, must often swim against the tide. Having been a silent witness to countless exchanges between Andrée and Karim, I can attest that these concerns were present from the conception of the book, and throughout its gestation. How do we innovate without turning away from tradition? How do we preserve heritage without stifling invention? How do we pass down our mothers' and grandmothers' words without disconcerting our daughters and sons, and at the same time be understood by the rest of the world? In other words, how do we respect the future without insulting the past – or vice versa? These are questions asked in every part of the world and in every area of life; but nowhere are the answers so comforting – or so delicious.

Introduction

Andrée Maalouf & Karim Haïdar

Lebanese cookery is at once famous and obscure. Although some of its dishes, humbly born in Beirut or a little-known village, have found their place on countless tables across the world, these do not sufficiently reflect the subtlety of its flavours nor the diversity of its inspirations: sometimes they even contribute to a truncated, simplistic and impoverished image of it.

This book's ambition is to shed light on the vast range of a very ancient culinary tradition, some of its recipes going back to biblical or Mesopotamian antiquity, but one which remains astonishingly alive and deserves to take its place among the great cuisines of the future.

In fact, Lebanese gastronomy contains numerous eastern influences – Egyptian, Syrian, Armenian, Turkish, Greek, Indian etc. – combined with local traditions that are equally numerous: traditions from a land of mountains, coasts, valleys and plains, where every town, every district and even every small village cultivates its individuality, its habits, its secrets; all the idiosyncrasies of a country made up of multiple religious communities which each have their own customs and festivals, and their dishes to celebrate them. What's more, in this gastronomic tradition, two powerful currents constantly run alongside each other without ever merging: home cookery and restaurant cookery.

This book aims to reveal some of these many facets. It is the work of two Lebanese people who are passionate about cooking and who for years have been looking to renew traditional recipes whilst retaining their authenticity. Karim Haïdar set aside a promising legal career to devote himself to his passion. In the restaurants he has managed, in Paris and London, he has shown an inventiveness that in the space of a few years has made him the standard-bearer for a resolutely contemporary Lebanese cuisine. This book contains the recipes that have made his name and reputation. In 2008, Karim opened a Lebanese seafood restaurant, La Branche d'Olivier, in Paris.

Andrée Maalouf comes from a long line of pastry cooks and confectioners, but it's in her own home that she presides, enthusiastically trying her hand at culinary experiments from every tradition, beginning with those of Lebanon. She derives great pleasure from uncovering a forgotten recipe, trying it out and then sharing it with others – endeavouring to preserve the flavours of the past, but also taking into account today's knowledge, especially as regards nutrition and health.

This book was born from their meeting. They have brought together their experience, their savoir faire, their own styles, sensibilities and memories – and their love of sharing and hospitality.

Mezze

The Image of Diversity

The word *mezze* refers to the series of hors d'oeuvres served at the beginning of a Lebanese meal. There are dozens of them, hot and cold, and they vary according to the region as much as the individual kitchen, reflecting the country's extreme diversity. Of course one can invent one's own and we certainly have, but some of the classics are indispensable. At a traditional meal, as soon as the guests sit down, they would expect to find on the table olives, bread and a large plate of crudités: cucumbers, radishes, peppers, tomatoes, spring onions, lettuce hearts, cabbage leaves etc. Then the different *mezze* arrive in successive waves, in an almost sacred order: first the salads, with *fattoush* and *tabbouleh* to the fore, then the various cold dishes: hummus, *moutabal*, stuffed vine leaves, lentil *moudardara* etc. Later come the hot dishes: falafel, pastry stuffed with Swiss chard, cheese and meat; fried Middle-Eastern cheeses etc. Some of the rarer old recipes and a few contemporary inventions are included in the following pages, alongside the classics.

LEBANESE SALADS

FATTOUSH

This is the archetypal peasant salad, featuring various garden herbs – purslane, mint, parsley and lettuce – as well as radish, tomato and cucumber. It also includes leftover bread, which is grilled and then broken up, and this breaking up or crumbling, called fatt, *gives the dish its name. Some people even add fried aubergine. As a final touch, it is important to sprinkle over a good few pinches of* sumac, *without which the Lebanese would not recognise the taste or appearance of their* fattoush.

PREPARATION: 30 MINS

SERVES 6

2 gem lettuces
or 1 romaine lettuce
250g cherry tomatoes
2 small cucumbers
(or half a large one)
½ bunch radishes
4 spring onions
1 bunch flat-leaf parsley
½ bunch of mint
2 pitta bread
150ml olive oil
50ml red wine vinegar
1 tablespoon *sumac*
(see p. 162)
Salt

1. Preheat oven to 150°C (gas mark 5).
2. Remove the leaves from the parsley and mint and roughly chop.
3. Slice the lettuces into strips, cut the cherry tomatoes in two vertically (or dice if using normal size tomatoes), slice the radishes and spring onions into rings and the unpeeled cucumbers into semi- circles.
4. Using scissors, cut the bread into 2cm wide squares, separate the two sides of each piece and grill them on a plate in the oven for 10 minutes.
5. Mix the bread with the olive oil and the *sumac*, which will keep the bread crispy.
6. Just before serving, toss all the ingredients with the bread and add vinegar and salt.

VARIATIONS

- A different Beiruti version leaves out the vinegar, parsley, mint and lettuce, compensating with more *sumac* and purslane; since the latter is often hard to find, it can be replaced with lamb's lettuce.
- In the mountains, *debs remmane* is used instead of vinegar (pomegranate molasses, see p. 166).

GOOD TO KNOW

- Traditionally, the skin of a cucumber is said to aid its digestion. If you like, you can peel it anyway, in alternate strips.
- You can prepare this salad ahead of time and season at the last minute.

TABBOULEH

The Lebanese have mixed feelings about tabbouleh's worldwide success. Though they are proud to see their national dish featured on a restaurant menu or on the shelves of a food shop, they find it hard to accept how radically it's been transformed and reconstituted until in their eyes it is barely recognisable. First off, its appearance: Lebanese tabbouleh is predominantly green and red, flecked with brown, while its homonym is predominantly yellow with a few red and green touches. This of course reflects the different ingredients: tabbouleh is made of parsley – a lot of parsley! – tomatoes and onion, as well as a little bulgur wheat, while its namesake is mostly couscous, scattered with a few sprigs of parsley and some diced tomato. Evidently there's been confusion, or a quid pro quo, between two very distinct Mediterranean traditions: one Levantine, from the Ottoman culinary universe, the other North African with its origins around Andalusia. Two great, time-honoured cuisines, each with its own spirit, techniques and specific ingredients, each of which deserves appreciation.

PREPARATION: 45 MINS

SERVES 6

3 tomatoes
3 spring onions
3 bunches flat-leaf parsley
1 bunch mint
2 tablespoons fine bulgur
wheat (see p. 160)
150ml lemon juice (3 lemons)
100ml olive oil
Salt

1. Wash the parsley and the mint. Leave to dry on kitchen paper.
2. Finely chop the onions and parsley and dice the tomatoes.
3. Place the bulgur wheat into a large salad bowl. Add the spring onions, tomatoes, parsley, lemon juice, olive oil and salt.
4. Remove the mint leaves and finely chop at the end, so they do not discolour.
5. Mix thoroughly then serve, with romaine lettuce leaves or Lebanese cabbage as accompaniment. You can prepare this salad in advance and season at the last minute.

 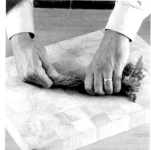  

KARIM'S TWIST

If you feel like innovating, you can blend in ½ a Granny Smith apple, cut into small cubes; purists will raise their eyebrows, but the crunchiness and acidity of the fruit combine well with the other ingredients.
You can also replace the mint with fresh coriander.

TOMATOES WITH CUMIN

PREPARATION: 10 MINS

COOLING: 30 MINS

SERVES 6

6 large very ripe tomatoes
3 teaspoons cumin powder
½ teaspoon caster sugar
Salt and pepper

1. Peel the tomatoes then cut into 2cm wide cubes.
2. Add the cumin, sugar, salt and pepper; combine. Leave somewhere cool for 30 minutes.
3. Serve with grilled meat or lentil purée.

VARIATION

- For a spicier taste, add 1 clove crushed garlic.

GOOD TO KNOW

- You can prepare this salad in advance and season at the last minute.

ARTICHOKE HEARTS AND BROAD BEAN SALAD

PREPARATION: 20 MINS

COOKING: 20 MINS

SERVES 6

12 artichoke hearts (fresh or frozen)
1kg green broad beans, fresh unshelled (or 400g frozen shelled broad beans)
6 spring onions
3 lemons and juice of ½ a lemon
100ml olive oil
Salt and pepper

1. Cook the artichoke hearts for 10 minutes in salted water, with a little lemon juice so they do not discolour.
2. Shell the beans; cook for 10 minutes in salted water; remove the second skin.
3. Peel the lemons, remove the pith and divide into segments (only the pulp should remain). Slice the onions into thin rings.
4. Mix together the broad beans, onion rings, lemon segments and olive oil. Season with salt and pepper.
5. Stuff the artichoke hearts with the mixture, then serve.

GOOD TO KNOW

- You can prepare this salad in advance and season at the last minute.

ROCKET WITH OLIVES

PREPARATION: 15 MINS

SERVES 6

300g (approx) rocket
6 spring onions
3 lemons
200g black olives
100ml olive oil
Salt and pepper

1. Wash and dry the rocket.
2. Finely chop the spring onions. Peel the lemons, remove the pith and divide into segments (only the pulp should remain). Stone the olives.
3. Combine the mixture with olive oil, salt and pepper and serve.

VARIATION

- You can substitute finely shredded savory for the rocket.

GOOD TO KNOW

- You can prepare this salad in advance and season at the last minute.

VEGETABLES

STUFFED VINE LEAVES

PREPARATION: 1HR
RESTING: 1HR
COOKING: 45 MINS

SERVES 6

70 vine leaves
2 potatoes
2 tomatoes
1 onion
2 bunches flat-leaf parsley
½ bunch mint
250ml lemon juice (about 4 lemons)
50g short-grain rice
150ml olive oil
Salt

1. Rinse the vine leaves thoroughly. Peel the onion.
2. Roughly chop the parsley, mint, onion and tomatoes then combine with the rice, lemon juice, olive oil and salt.
3. Leave to rest for 1 hour at room temperature or in the fridge, then place the mixture in a sieve over a large bowl to catch the juice.
4. Peel the potatoes and cut them into round slices 1cm thick.
5. Place them around the base of a large saucepan.
6. Lay 1 vine leaf on your work surface, fill and seal it (see illustrated steps below).
7. Follow the same procedure with 59 of the vine leaves.
8. Stack the stuffed vine leaves side by side in the saucepan, in several layers, on top of the potatoes.
9. Cover with the remaining 10 leaves (unstuffed).
10. Add the juice collected from the mixture as well as water to cover and simmer gently for 45 minutes, covered. The cooking time will vary depending on the quality of the vine leaves: they should melt in the mouth.
11. Serve cold.

VARIATIONS

- You can use fresh vine leaves for this recipe; just blanch before use to soften.
- Swiss chard is sometimes used instead of vine leaves; if you use it, add a handful of chickpeas to the stuffing.

GOOD TO KNOW

- You can find vine leaves in many of the large supermarkets or in specialist shops (see p. 170).

  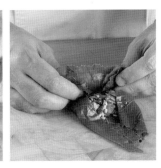 

OKRA WITH OLIVE OIL

BEMIEH BZEIT

PREPARATION: 25 MINS
COOKING: 30 MINS

SERVES 6

1kg small okra, fresh or
frozen
3 ripe tomatoes
2 onions
1 whole garlic bulb
3 tablespoons olive oil
Salt

1. If the okra are fresh, cut away the conical cap from the stalk end, but be sure not to pierce the okra or they will turn sticky. Sauté in a little olive oil and reserve. If the okra are frozen, use as is.
2. Peel and chop the onions, peel the garlic. Blanch and peel the tomatoes and cut into quarters.
3. In a large casserole, sauté the onions for a few minutes with the remainder of the olive oil. Add the okra, tomatoes and whole garlic cloves. Season with salt.
4. Cover and leave to simmer gently for 20 minutes.
5. Serve.

VARIATION

- After cooking, sprinkle with snips of fresh coriander.

GREEN BEANS WITH OLIVE OIL

PREPARATION: 20 MINS
COOKING: 20 MINS

SERVES 6

1kg green beans, preferably
runner beans
3 very ripe tomatoes
2 onions
1 whole garlic bulb
3 tablespoons olive oil
Salt

1. Cut the beans into three or four sections, diagonally, and cut off the ends.
2. Peel and thinly slice the onions.
3. Peel the tomatoes and chop into eight chunks.
4. Peel the garlic cloves.
5. In a frying pan, sauté the onions for 5 minutes in olive oil. Add the beans and stir until their colour deepens. Add the garlic and tomato, season with salt, and simmer for 20 minutes, covered.
6. Serve warm or cold, as a starter or with grilled meat.

AUBERGINE MAGHMOUR

PREPARATION: 30 MINS

SOAKING: 1 NIGHT

COOKING: 45 MINS

SERVES 6

3 aubergines
2 carrots
1 large, very ripe tomato
1 onion
1 head of garlic
1 handful chickpeas
1 litre frying oil
Salt

THE DAY BEFORE

1. Peel the aubergines. Cut them in two widthways, then each half into four. Sprinkle generously with salt and leave to drain in a colander in the fridge.
2. Soak the chickpeas in 1 litre lukewarm water.

ON THE DAY

3. Deep-fry the aubergines for 4 minutes.
4. Lay them on kitchen paper and reserve a little of the oil.
5. Cook the chickpeas in the water from cold. Do not add salt. Count 30 minutes from boiling, then run under cold water and rub with your hands to remove the skins.
6. Peel the onion and slice into strips.
7. Peel and de-seed the tomato; cut into eight pieces.
8. Peel the carrots and cut into juliennes (thin batons).
9. Peel the garlic cloves.
10. In a saucepan, sauté the strips of onion in 2 tablespoons of the frying oil. Add the carrot batons, the garlic cloves, tomato and finally the chickpeas.
11. Place the chunks of aubergine on top of the mixture, leaving no gaps. Place a weight, such as an overturned plate, on top, to hold them in place. Add enough water to cover the aubergines. Simmer gently, covered, for 15 minutes.
12. Turn out on to a plate and serve warm or cold, as a starter.

GOOD TO KNOW

•   Choose the aubergines carefully, favouring black over reddish-black skin, and trying to pick small, light aubergines so they have as few seeds as possible.

COOKING WITH SESAME

In the cuisine of Lebanon and its surrounding region, no ingredient is more ubiquitous than this little oily seed with its subtle flavours, which lends its ivory colour to so many famous dishes, such as hummus and *moutabal*, tarator and tajine sauces.

MOUTABAL

The word moutabal *simply means 'seasoned', a term that can be used of many dishes; but in its simplest form,* moutabal *itself is an aubergine purée blended with tahini, the sesame paste.*

PREPARATION: IO MINS

COOKING: 40 MINS

SERVES 6

3 aubergines
1 garlic clove
Juice of 1 lemon
2 tablespoons *tahini* (sesame paste, see p. 167)
Pomegranate seeds
Salt

1. Score the skin of the aubergines several times with a knife.
2. Place the aubergines on an ovenproof tray; grill in the oven with the door open and turn so that the skin all over is lightly charred and the flesh is soft.
3. Rinse the aubergines in cold water. Holding them by their stalks, make an incision along the length. Delicately remove the flesh and leave to drain in a sieve. Keep the skins.
4. Reduce the aubergine flesh to a purée using a pestle or a fork.
5. Peel and crush the garlic and mix with the *tahini*, lemon juice and the aubergine flesh. Add salt and stir again.
6. Carefully fill the aubergine skins and serve, sprinkled with pomegranate seeds.

VARIATIONS

- You can add 2 tablespoons yoghurt.
- You can also use *debs remmane* (pomegranate molasses, see p. 166) in place of lemon juice.
- You can serve the *moutabal* in a small bowl, and discard the aubergine skins.

GOOD TO KNOW

- If you use a food processor for this recipe, only whizz a few times to purée the aubergine, otherwise the mixture will be too thin.

COURGETTES MOUTABAL

PREPARATION: 10 MINS

COOKING: 20 MINS

SERVES 6

6 courgettes
Juice of 1 lemon
1 garlic clove
2 tablespoons *tahini* (sesame paste, see p. 167)
30g pine nuts (see p. 163)
½ teaspoon 7 Spice Mix (see p. 165)
Salt

1. Preheat the oven to 200°C (gas mark 6–7).
2. Remove the tops of the courgettes. Cut them in two lengthways and place in an ovenproof dish.
3. Put in the oven and bake for 20 minutes.
4. Peel and crush the garlic.
5. Mash the courgettes, add the garlic, lemon juice, *tahini* and 7 Spice Mix; add salt and mix thoroughly.
6. Dry-roast the pine nuts in a pan until golden, and add to mixture.
7. Serve warm or cold, with other *mezze* or as a garnish for white meat.

GOOD TO KNOW

- You can use yellow courgettes, which are more floury and contain less water.

SWISS CHARD MOUTABAL

This recipe is prepared with the stalks of the chard used in the Lentil Soup with Swiss Chard and Lemon (see p. 52). Otherwise, use the stalks of about ten chard.

PREPARATION: 10 MINS

COOKING: 40 MINS

SERVES 6

10 chard stalks
150ml lemon juice
500ml milk
4 tablespoons *tahini* (sesame paste, see p. 167)
Salt

1. Wash and chop the chard stalks into 1cm sections.
2. Simmer the chard stalks in equal parts water and milk for around 40 minutes until they are soft. Drain.
3. Mix the *tahini* with the lemon juice and a little water to produce a cream; stir in the chard and add salt.
4. Serve.

VARIATION

- You can also pound all the ingredients with a pestle to make a chard cream, which is the perfect accompaniment for fish.

GOOD TO KNOW

- You can use water with a dash of lemon in place of the milk so that the chard does not discolour.

TAHINI-BASED SAUCES

TARATOR SAUCE

This is a lemon-flavoured sauce, ideal with fish or falafel.

PREPARATION: 5 MINS

FOR 300ML SAUCE

4 tablespoons *tahini* (sesame paste, see p. 167)
100ml lemon juice
100ml water
1 garlic clove
Salt

1. Peel and crush the garlic. Add the *tahini*, lemon juice, salt and water.
2. Stir gently until it attains the consistency of smooth cream.
3. If the mixture shrinks, add 1 tablespoon water and continue stirring.

VARIATIONS

- You can mix in ½ a bunch of flat-leaf parsley, finely shredded.
- You can blend 100g pine nuts (see p. 163) in a food processor and add them to the sauce.
- It's also possible to use bitter orange juice instead of lemon juice or, if it isn't the season for bitter oranges, a mixture of grapefruit, orange and lemon or mandarin. Do not, of course, exceed the required amount.

TAJINE SAUCE

Tajine in Lebanese cookery is a hot tahini-based sauce. A cousin of tarator but far more rare, it's traditionally cooked in the oven in an earthenware dish and goes very well with fish.

PREPARATION: 10 MINS

COOKING: 20 MINS

FOR 500ML SAUCE

2 onions
6 tablespoons *tahini* (sesame paste, see p. 167)
150ml lemon or bitter orange juice
150ml water
2 tablespoons vegetable oil
Salt

1. Strip the onions of their outer skins and chop finely. Sauté in oil on a low heat but do not allow to colour.
2. Whisk the *tahini*, water, lemon juice and salt. Add this mixture to the onions.
3. Cook over a low heat in the frying pan until the *tahini*'s oil rises to the surface.
4. Serve hot.

VARIATIONS

- You can add roasted pine nuts (see p. 163).
- Traditionally, fish and Tajine Sauce would be cooked together in an earthenware bowl in the oven.

HUMMUS

Together with tabbouleh, *the chickpea purée hummus is undoubtedly the best-known dish in Lebanese cookery. It's also the one that provokes the liveliest arguments; it's not uncommon to hear amateur cooks boast of knowing the only way to achieve a smooth hummus. Chickpeas should be cooked according to their quality: the best are big and covered in little bumps. They only need to be put to soak the day before and then cooked in a pressure cooker in unsalted water; they will soften and be ready for use. When the chickpeas are of lesser quality, small and smooth, add 1 teaspoon bicarbonate of soda to the soaking water.*

PREPARATION: 20 MINS

SOAKING: 1 NIGHT

COOKING: 2 HRS

SERVES 8

250g chickpeas
1 garlic clove
150ml lemon juice
6 tablespoons *tahini* (sesame paste, see p. 167)
A drizzle of olive oil
Salt

KARIM'S TWIST

If you want to surprise your guests, replace part of the lemon juice with orange-blossom water (see p. 169).

THE DAY BEFORE

1. Soak the chickpeas in 4 times their volume of unsalted water.

ON THE DAY

2. Rinse the chickpeas and cook in a pressure cooker for 2 hrs.
3. Drain and reserve the cooking water.
4. Peel the garlic and blend in a food processor for 2 or 3 minutes, then add the *tahini*, lemon juice, chickpeas and salt.
5. Blend for 10 minutes, gradually adding the cooking water until the consistency of a purée is achieved.
6. Check the seasoning and add olive oil.
7. Eat with pitta bread. This dish goes very well with Grilled Kaftah as well as Shish Taouk (see p. 94 and p. 98)

VARIATIONS

- You can omit the garlic (some purists assert that a good hummus never contains garlic) and reduce the lemon juice to a minimum.
- Some Beirutis add finely shredded parsley and chilli powder.
- You can serve this dish with *awarma* lamb confit (sold ready made in Middle-Eastern food shops) and roasted pine nuts (see p. 163).

GOOD TO KNOW

- Especially when made without garlic, hummus can be kept in the fridge for 2 days.

COMMENT

Some people remove the skins from the chickpeas before blending, and restaurants add oil at the very end, whipping up the hummus like a mayonnaise to make it smoother.

PULSES

Several pulses play a very important role in Lebanese cuisine. This is clearly true for chickpeas, which are used for the indispensable hummus, and for broad beans (fava beans), which are the main ingredient of falafel, one of our most popular dishes. Various dishes containing these two pulses – as well as dried haricot beans – sometimes constitute families' only meal of the day, accompanied by a salad. Lentils, too, are fundamental to Lebanese cooking and have been used in recipes since ancient times.

MOUDARDARA

YELLOW LENTIL SALAD

PREPARATION: 15 MINS

COOKING: 45 MINS

SERVES 6

400g yellow lentils
100g basmati rice
4 onions
600ml frying oil
Salt

1. Peel the onions, cut in half vertically then slice thinly into half moons.
2. Pour the oil into a frying pan. When it's hot, add the onions.
3. Stir constantly until the onions are golden and crispy. Remove from the pan and lay out on kitchen paper to drain excess oil. Leave the onions to cool and reserve the cooking oil.
4. Place the lentils in a saucepan and add 4 times their volume of unsalted water. Bring to the boil and simmer for 20 minutes.
5. Strain the lentils, reserving their cooking liquid.
6. Sauté the rice in 100ml of the onions' cooking oil until it turns translucent. Add twice its volume of water, using the lentils' cooking liquid. Season generously with salt. Bring to the boil. Simmer very gently for 7 minutes.
7. Add the lentils, cover and simmer for 4 minutes.
8. Remove and leave covered for a further 15 minutes, so that the rice continues to swell. Leave to cool.
9. Once the mixture has cooled, stir so that the grains do not split.
10. Decorate the plate with the crispy onions. Eat chilled or at room temperature with a tomato salad (Tomatoes with Cumin, p. 18).

VARIATION

- In South Lebanon, slices or quarters of peeled oranges are added.

MOUJADDARA

A BIBLICAL DISH

It was for a plate of lentils that Esau sold his birthright to his brother Jacob. It's not too far-fetched to believe that the dish in question was an ancient version of moujaddara, *which seems to date back to the dawn of time, although we find other lentil-based dishes in Middle-Eastern cookery – soups, purées, salads etc.*

There are different kinds of lentils for different recipes. Green lentils or 'coral' lentils (red lentils with the skins removed) are best for moujaddara.

In Middle-Eastern dishes, rice is associated with lentils. Some nutritionists believe that, in order to be able to assimilate the protein in lentils, chickpeas or dried haricot beans, the body needs them to be combined with a grain such as rice, wheat (contained in bread) or bulgur wheat.

PREPARATION: 15 MINS

COOKING: 45 MINS

SERVES 6

400g green or coral lentils
100g short-grain rice
4 onions
100ml olive oil
Salt

1. Rinse the lentils and the rice separately.
2. Place the lentils in a saucepan and add 4 times their volume in unsalted water. Bring to the boil and simmer for 20 minutes.
3. Blend the mixture and strain or sieve. Put to one side.
4. Peel and finely chop the onions. Sauté in a pan with the olive oil until golden.
5. Pour the lentil purée into a saucepan, add the onions, rice and salt. Cover and simmer for 25 minutes, until the rice is cooked through and the consistency is even.
6. Serve cold with a cabbage or tomato salad.

VARIATION

• You may leave the lentils unblended and add the rice after cooking for 10 minutes, followed by the onion.

CORAL LENTIL MOUJADDARA

PREPARATION: 15 MINS

COOKING: 40 MINS

SERVES 6

400g coral lentils

100g short-grain rice

4 onions

100ml olive oil

Salt

1. Rinse the lentils and the rice together in a sieve.
2. Peel and finely chop the onions. In a saucepan, fry the onions gently in olive oil until they turn golden.
3. Add the lentils and rice, cover with water leaving a 2cm gap between the water and the rim of the pan.
4. Bring to the boil and simmer for around 30 minutes, covered, stirring occasionally.
5. After 30 minutes, add salt and continue to heat and stir until the mixture attains the consistency of a purée.
6. Serve hot or cold with a salad.

FALAFEL

Of Egyptian origin, falafel are small balls made from pulses, chickpeas and broad beans (also called fava beans), ground, uncooked, and mixed with spices, fresh parsley and fresh coriander, then fried in oil. They are often served at roadside stalls where people cluster and watch them being fried, waiting for them to be handed over, wrapped in bread, with a mixture of thinly sliced raw vegetables and a good dash of tarator sauce.

PREPARATION: 10 MINS

SOAKING: 1 NIGHT

COOKING: 20 MINS

TO MAKE 50 BALLS

250g chickpeas
250g dried broad beans
2 garlic cloves
1 leek
½ courgette
1 bunch coriander
1 tablespoon powdered
falafel spices:
¼ black pepper
½ coriander
¼ cinnamon
1 teaspoon bicarbonate of
soda
Frying oil
Salt

FOR THE GARNISH

3 tomatoes or 10 cherry
tomatoes
1 bunch radishes
1 bunch mint
1 bunch flat-leaf parsley
Pickled turnips (see facing
page)

THE DAY BEFORE

1. Soak the chickpeas and broad beans in a large container with 3 times their volume of water.

ON THE DAY

2. Clean the leek and cut into large sections. Peel the garlic; remove the coriander leaves from the stems. Cut the courgette into chunks.
3. Strain the chickpeas and broad beans and blend, uncooked, with the leek, garlic, coriander and the courgette.
4. Add the spices, salt and bicarbonate and blend well. The mixture should remain firm and smooth.
5. Shape into small balls 4cm in diameter. Fry for 6 to 7 minutes in a deep-fryer at 150°C.
6. Serve with Tarator Sauce (see p. 29), pickled turnips and the garnish (tomatoes, radish, parsley and mint, finely chopped).

VARIATIONS

- You can add different ingredients, like chilli, pepper or dill to the blending mixture, or omit others, for example the leek or courgette.
- You can also omit the bicarbonate of soda, in which case the falafel will be denser, containing less air.

PICKLED TURNIPS

PREPARATION: 10 MINS

MARINADE: 1 WEEK

FOR A 700ML JAR

2 bunches baby turnips
200ml red wine vinegar
150ml water
1 tablespoon coarse salt

1. Wash the turnips and cut off their stalks.
2. Place in a jar, packing tightly.
3. Add vinegar, salt and water to completely cover the turnips.
4. Seal the jar and wait one week before consuming.

VARIATIONS

- You can use cider vinegar for this recipe, making the vinegary taste milder.
- You can cut a deep cross into each turnip, which will speed up the pickling process.
- A chunk of beetroot is customarily added to give a beautiful red colour.

GOOD TO KNOW

- You can find pickled turnips in Middle-Eastern food shops.

MOUAJANATS

Several dishes characteristic of the cooking of Lebanon and its region are called *mouajanats*, derived from *ajeen*, which means pastry. There is *lahm bi ajeen*, 'meat on dough', a kind of meat pizza; *sambousik*, the name recalling Indian samosa, which refers to pastry stuffed with cheese or meat and rolled into half-moon shapes; *fatayers*, which are triangular and stuffed with spinach or chard; *rekakats*, made with very fine pastry, and we must not forget *mana'ish*, which are eaten at all hours of the day, but mostly at breakfast.

MANA'ISH

ROUND FLAT BREAD WITH ZAATAR

PREPARATION: 20 MINS

RESTING: 40 MINS

COOKING: 7 MINS

TO MAKE 6 MANA'ISH

FOR THE DOUGH

400g plain white flour
1 tablespoon olive oil
1 sachet baker's yeast
½ teaspoon salt
1 teaspoon sugar

FOR THE FILLING

60g *zaatar* (see p. 164)
200ml olive oil

1. Combine the *zaatar* and the olive oil in a bowl.
2. Dissolve the yeast in 250ml lukewarm water. Place the flour, olive oil, salt, sugar, and the water and yeast mixture in a food processor. Pulse slowly for a few minutes. The dough should come away from the sides; if it does not, add 1 tablespoon flour.
3. Remove the dough from the processor, sprinkle with a little flour so it does not stick to your hands, place on a work surface, divide into 6 equal parts, cover and leave to rise for at least 30 minutes.
4. Once risen, lay out the 6 dough balls, flatten to a circle shape and pinch the edges. Press your fingers into the surface 5 or 6 times.
5. Preheat the oven to 210°C (gas mark 7).
6. Place 2 tablespoons of the *zaatar* and oil mixture in the centre of each circle, and spread evenly. Place on a baking tray covered in greaseproof paper. Leave to rest for 10 minutes.
7. Cook in the oven for 10 minutes.
8. Serve immediately.

COMMENTS

• For all bread and pastry recipes, it is best to use organic flour as it contains more fibre. You can substitute wholemeal flour for part of the plain white flour in this recipe; a little bran retains moisture and prevents the pastry drying out. You could also mix the white flour with spelt flour or fine wheat semolina, which will make it lighter. Untreated flours are ideal.

REKAKATS

PASTRY WRAPS WITH CHEESE AND PARSLEY

PREPARATION: 15 MINS

COOKING: 5 MINS

SERVES 6

6 brik or filo sheets
1 halloumi cheese (see p. 46)
1 bunch flat-leaf parsley

1. Blend the cheese and parsley.
2. Cut 10cm squares into the brik or filo sheets.
3. Place 1 tablespoon of the mixture in the middle of each square of pastry. Fold 1cm at opposite ends, then roll up, squeezing tightly so that filling does not escape.
4. Fry the *rekakats* in a pan or cook for 5 minutes in a preheated oven at 210ºC (gas mark 7).
5. Serve.

COMMENTS

• Filo is a very fine pastry made from flour and water. One packet contains several dozen rectangular sheets, used for various oriental pastries such as baklava. They can also be used in savoury cooking. Filo sheets can be kept for 2 or 3 days in the fridge, covered in a damp cloth, or in the freezer. Brik is thicker, but it can be used instead of filo in some recipes, such as *rekakats*.

• You will find halloumi in Middle-Eastern food shops. This ewe's milk cheese is originally from Cyprus but made in Denmark, Greece etc.

VARIATIONS

• You can stuff the *rekakats* with a mixture of meat, onions and pine nuts (see p. 163).

• You can also replace the halloumi with a mixture of 150g feta cheese and 100g mozzarella

SAMBOUSIKS

TO MAKE 6 SAMBOUSIKS

FOR THE PASTRY

200mg plain white flour
2 tablespoons olive oil
1 pinch salt
½ teaspoon caster sugar

FOR THE FILLING

100g minced lamb
100g onions
20g pine nuts (see p. 163)
1 tablespoon yoghurt
A few leaves of flat-leaf
parsley
A little vegetable oil
Salt and pepper

FILLING

1. Peel and chop the onions, sauté in a little oil.
2. Dry-roast the pine nuts in a pan.
3. Add the lamb and pine nuts to the onions.
4. Cook for 10 minutes over a low heat.
5. Meanwhile, chop the parsley leaves.
6. Add salt, pepper, remove from heat and add the yoghurt and chopped parsley.

PASTRY

7. Place the flour, oil, salt, caster sugar and 150ml water in a food processor.
8. Pulse slowly in a food processor for a few minutes. The dough should come away from the sides; if it does not, add 1 tablespoon flour.
9. Take the pastry out of the food processor, sprinkle with a little flour so it does not stick to your hands, place on a work surface, cover and leave to rise for at least 30 minutes.
10. Preheat the oven to 200ºC (gas mark 6–7).
11. Generously flour the work surface, flatten the pastry by hand, turn over and flatten again with a rolling pin.
12. Cut out 6 circles 8cm in diameter. Divide the filling into 6 equal amounts and place on the pastry discs.
13. Slightly dampen the edges and seal the *sambousiks* in half-moon shapes, pressing the ends with a fork. Arrange on a baking tray covered in greaseproof paper.
14. Cook in the oven for 10 minutes.
15. Serve immediately.

COMMENTS

- For all bread and pastry recipes, it is best to use organic flour as it contains more fibre. You can substitute wholemeal flour for part of the plain white flour in this recipe; a little bran retains moisture and prevents the pastry drying out. You could also mix the white flour with spelt flour or fine wheat semolina, which will make it lighter. Untreated flours are ideal.

VARIATION

- You can replace the filling with grated halloumi cheese and chopped parsley.

LAHM BI AJEEN

SMALL LAMB AND TOMATO TARTS

PREPARATION: 10 MINS

RESTING: 45 MINS

COOKING: 7 MINS

SERVES 6

FOR THE PASTRY

400g plain white flour

1 teaspoon caster sugar

1 sachet baker's yeast

½ teaspoon salt

1 tablespoon olive oil

FOR THE FILLING

200g minced lamb

250g tomatoes

¼ onion

A few drops of *debs remmane* (pomegranate molasses, see p. 166)

Salt and pepper

To accompany: natural yoghurt

PASTRY

1. Dissolve the yeast in 250ml warm water.
2. Place the flour, sugar, oil, salt and yeast mixture in a food processor.
3. Pulse slowly in a food processor for a few minutes. The dough should come away from the sides; if it does not, add 1 tablespoon flour.
4. Take the dough out of the processor, sprinkle with a little flour to stop it sticking to your hands, place on a work surface, divide into 6 equal parts, cover and leave to rise for at least 30 minutes.
5. Generously flour the work surface. Flatten the 6 dough balls by hand, turn over and flatten again with a rolling pin. Cut out 6 circles, 8cm in diameter, and lay on a baking tray covered in greaseproof paper.
6. Leave for 15 minutes.

FILLING

7. Preheat the oven to 200ºC (gas mark 6–7)
8. Blend the tomatoes and the onion with salt and pepper, add a few drops of *debs remmane*. With a fork or pestle, combine with the minced meat.
9. Divide the filling among the pastry circles and spread evenly.
10. Cook in oven for 7 minutes.
11. Serve with yoghurt.

COMMENTS

- For all bread and pastry recipes, it is best to use organic flour as it contains more fibre. You can substitute wholemeal flour for part of the plain white flour in this recipe; a little bran retains moisture and prevents the pastry drying out. You could also mix the white flour with spelt flour or fine wheat semolina, which will make it lighter. Untreated flours are ideal.

FATAYERS WITH SPINACH

PREPARATION: 10 MINS

RESTING: 30 MINS

COOKING: 15 MINS

TO MAKE 6 FATAYERS

FOR THE FILLING

200g fresh spinach

50g onions

20g pine nuts (see p. 163)

100ml lemon juice

50ml olive oil

1 tablespoon *sumac*

(see p. 162)

Salt

FOR THE PASTRY

200g plain white flour

½ teaspoon caster sugar

½ sachet baker's yeast

1 tablespoon olive oil

A pinch of salt

FILLING

1. Peel the onions. Chop the spinach and the onions.
2. In a pan, dry-roast the pine nuts until golden.
3. Mix the spinach, onions, roasted pine nuts, lemon juice, salt, olive oil and *sumac*. Put to one side.

PASTRY

4. Dissolve the yeast in 150ml lukewarm water.
5. Place the flour, olive oil, sugar, salt, water and yeast in a food processor.
6. Blend on a low speed for 15 minutes. The dough should come away from the sides; if it does not, add a tablespoon of flour.
7. Take the dough out of the processor, dust with a little flour so it does not stick to your hands, place on a work surface, cover and leave to rise for at least 30 minutes.
8. Preheat the oven to 200°C (gas mark 6–7).
9. Generously flour the work surface, flatten the pastry with your fingers, turn it over and flatten again using a rolling pin.
10. Cut out 6 circles, 8cm in diameter, and arrange on a baking tray covered in greaseproof paper. Divide the filling into 6 equal parts and spread on to the pastry circles.
11. Dampen the edges and fold over to form a triangle, pinching to seal.
12. Cook in the oven for 10 minutes.
13. Serve immediately.

VARIATION

- Fatayers with Swiss chard: use chard leaves instead of spinach.

LEBANESE CHEESES

Although there aren't many of them, cheeses have a special place in the Lebanese kitchen. Some, like *labneh*, are almost always on the table; others, like *shanklish*, require sophisticated preparation. Some cheeses are thought of as local even if they come from abroad, such as halloumi (originally from Cyprus) or *kashkawan*, sometimes called *kashkaval*, the name a local adaptation of the Italian *caciocavallo*. There are also mountain shepherds' traditional cheeses, or those from the Bekaa plain, which are curd cheeses made from goat's, cow's or ewe's milk. The Lebanese enjoy cheeses at all hours of the day – on waking, at the start of a meal, at teatime or whenever they feel peckish. On the other hand, it's not the custom to eat cheese at the end of the meal, between main course and dessert, as in France.

SHANKLISH IN SALAD

This recipe is named after a traditional cheese shaped into a spicy ball. This salad can be made using shanklish, *but since* shanklish *is not easy to find, other cheeses such as feta may be substituted.* Shanklish *is rare because the production process takes a long time and the tradition is dying out. In the past, when ewe's milk was churned to extract the cream and the butter, the liquid left over, called buttermilk, was used to make* shanklish. *This liquid was then boiled and strained and the curds obtained were salted, rolled into balls and left to dry in the sun. The cheeses were then placed in jars until they were covered in mould. They were then washed in water and placed out in the sun again. Next, various condiments were added: mint,* zaatar, *chilli, pepper, sometimes even nuts or garlic.*

PREPARATION: 30 MINS

STRAINING: 7 DAYS

SERVES 6

FOR THE CHEESE

500g *labneh* (see p. 49)
5 tablespoons *zaatar* (see p. 164)
1 tablespoon chilli powder

FOR THE GARNISH

250g cherry tomatoes
6 spring onions
15 basil leaves
Olive oil

SHANKLISH

1. Mix the *labneh*, the chilli powder and half the *zaatar*; divide into two equal parts and lay each on a tea towel over a plate.
2. Leave to strain for 3 days in the fridge, changing the tea towel regularly.
3. Shape each half into a ball and roll it in the remaining *zaatar*. Put it back to dry in the fridge for another four days.
4. This cheese can be stored for several weeks if kept in the fridge.

SALAD

5. Crumble the two balls of cheese, cut the tomatoes into quarters, chop the spring onions and the basil, mix all of it with a little olive oil and eat with bread as a *mezze*.

VARIATION

- You can replace *labneh* with feta; it is a drier cheese and you don't have to strain it for 7 days but can prepare the *shanklish* salad immediately.

FRIED HALLOUMI

PREPARATION: 5 MINS

SOAKING: 1 HR

COOKING: 5 MINS

SERVES 6

2 halloumi cheeses, 250g
each
1 teaspoon sesame seeds

KARIM'S TWIST
You can serve halloumi with
quince jam.

1. Cut the cheese into slices 1cm thick.
2. Place them to soak in cold water for 1 hour.
3. Drain and sear for 1 minute per side in a non-stick pan.
4. Scatter with sesame seeds, serve hot.

LABNEH

Labneh is a strained yoghurt which resembles fromage frais, which the Lebanese eat at different times of day – at breakfast, tea time, with mezze and sometimes even as a light supper. Usually drizzled with olive oil, it can be spread on bread with the addition of an olive, a little zaatar (see p. 164), a quarter of tomato, a slice of cucumber and a mint leaf, according to taste. Labneh is often the basis of the Lebanese 'sandwich' known as arouss – bread tightly rolled up with various ingredients. It is nourishing and easy to eat; you often see kids taking a bite without interrupting their games.

In the past, yoghurt and labneh were made every week in the home. Today, Lebanese people are more likely to buy dairy products in 'crèmeries' or large supermarkets. But some families still make them at home in the traditional way. After the milk is boiled, it is poured into an earthenware bowl called an edreh, which is glazed on the inside and left to cool.

For this recipe to work, it is essential that the milk be hot but not too hot. Brave cooks test it with their little finger: if you can count to 10 without burning yourself the milk is the right temperature. Then you mix in a small pot of yoghurt, cover the container with a plate wrapped in a thick cloth, and leave it to rest for a night. In the morning, the yoghurt is ready.

To transform it into labneh, pour into a muslin cloth, hang and leave to strain. A few hours later, take it down and you have a solid cheese. Add salt and store in the fridge. It can be kept this way for a week.

PREPARATION: 5 MINS

STRAINING: 1 NIGHT

SERVES 6

1kg whole or half-fat yoghurt
1 teaspoon salt

THE DAY BEFORE

1. Mix the yoghurt and salt together and place in a muslin cloth.
2. Place the cloth in a sieve.

ON THE DAY

3. Remove the curds and place somewhere cool.
4. Serve on bread with olive oil, *zaatar* (see p. 164) or mint leaves and cucumber.

VARIATIONS

- You can use ewe's milk yoghurt, which gives the *labneh* a smoother texture.
- You can also add all kinds of seasoning: dried mint, garlic etc.

SOUPS

There are countless soups in Lebanese cuisine, sometimes constituting
an evening meal in themselves. They often contain lentils
and other pulses and are rarely blended.

ADAS BI HAMOD

LENTIL SOUP WITH SWISS CHARD AND LEMON

Literally translated as 'lemon lentils', this village soup is a winter classic. It is usually served piping hot, but because of the ingredients used it can be served warm or even cold in all seasons.

PREPARATION: 25 MINS

COOKING: 40–45 MINS

SERVES 8

300g yellow lentils
2 potatoes
1 bunch of Swiss chard or 5 leaves
3 garlic cloves
3 onions
1 bunch coriander
Juice of 1 lemon
½ teaspoon cumin powder
2 tablespoons vegetable oil
Salt and pepper

1. Peel the onions and the garlic. Finely chop the onions and coriander separately.
2. Crush the garlic.
3. Peel the potatoes and cut into small cubes.
4. Wash and coarsely chop the chard leaves, keeping the stalks for another recipe, for example Swiss Chard Moutabal (see p. 28).
5. Pour 2 litres of water into a large casserole and cook the lentils for 30 minutes, covered.
6. Sauté the onions in a pan with the oil, add the garlic and then the coriander.
7. Add the chard and potatoes to the lentils, as well as the sautéed onion, garlic and coriander.
8. Cover and simmer 10 to 15 minutes.
9. Add cumin, salt, pepper and lemon juice.

VARIATIONS

- You can use green lentils for this recipe and you can include the chard stalks. If you do, they must be finely chopped so that they cook at the same time as the other ingredients; anticipate 5 minutes extra cooking time.
- You can add 4 small courgettes. Cut in half lengthways and chop into slices, 4mm thick.
- After cooking, you can also add 1 tablespoon flour, dissolved in water, to thicken the soup.
- In the Akkar region, red lentils are used for this recipe and a stick of cinnamon and mild pepper substituted for cumin.

CORAL LENTIL SOUP WITH TOMATO

PREPARATION: 5 MINS

COOKING: 20 MINS

SERVES 6

300g coral lentils
750ml tomato juice
1 bunch coriander
Salt

1. Rinse the lentils.
2. Place in a large casserole, add 750ml water and the tomato juice, cover and bring to the boil.
3. Simmer for 20 minutes.
4. While the lentils are cooking, finely shred the fresh coriander.
5. Season and serve the soup sprinkled with coriander.

VARIATION

- After cooking, add 2 garlic cloves, peeled and crushed.

YELLOW LENTIL SOUP

PREPARATION: 10 MINS

COOKING: 40 MINS

SERVES 6

400g yellow lentils
1 carrot
1 potato
250g minced lamb
Vegetable oil
Salt and pepper

1. Rinse the lentils. Peel the carrot and the potato.
2. Pour 1.5 litres water into a large casserole, add the lentils, the whole carrot and whole potato, bring to the boil then simmer for 30 minutes.
3. Blend the soup together and strain through a fine sieve. Add salt.
4. Season the meat with salt and pepper, shape into small balls and fry in a pan with a little oil.
5. Place the meatballs in the soup and bring to the boil.
6. Serve immediately.

VARIATION

- You can also serve this soup with croutons, fried or grilled, scattered over the top.

CHICKEN SOUP WITH VERMICELLI

PREPARATION: 10 MINS

COOKING: 1 HR

SERVES 6

1 chicken

200g vermicelli

2 onions

Juice of ½ a lemon

6 sprigs of flat-leaf parsley

4 tablespoons vegetable oil

Salt and pepper

1. Place the whole chicken in a saucepan with 2 tablespoons oil and sear until golden brown all over.
2. Meanwhile, peel the onions and cut into quarters.
3. Add 2 litres of water to the pan, add the onions and cook for 45 minutes.
4. Skim the surface several times to remove froth from the stock.
5. Remove the chicken and onions from the stock and leave to cool.
6. Remove the chicken's skin and bones; add the flesh to the stock.
7. In a pan, sauté the vermicelli in 2 tablespoons of oil until golden.
8. Add the vermicelli to the soup and cook for 10 minutes. Finely shred the parsley.
9. Season with salt and pepper and serve.
10. Sprinkle the bowls with the chopped parsley and serve with a dash of lemon juice on top.

HAMISS

SWEET ONION SOUP

PREPARATION: 40 MINS

COOKING: 35 MINS

SERVES 6

18 mini meat *kibbeh*, fried
(see p. 63)

2 kg onions

1 bunch flat-leaf parsley

1 litre water or chicken stock

2 tablespoons *debs remmane*
(pomegranate molasses, see
p. 166)

Salt

1. Peel the onions. Cook in salted water or chicken stock, covered, for 30 minutes. Blend in a food processor.
2. Add the kibbeh and bring to the boil.
3. Simmer for 5 minutes.
4. Add the *debs remmane*.
5. Sprinkle with finely shredded parsley before serving.

COMMENT

•   To make the mini *kibbeh*, follow the recipe on p. 63, shaping into small balls 3cm in diameter.

WINTER VEGETABLE SOUP

PREPARATION: 30 MINS

COOKING: 1 HR 20 MINS

SERVES 8

2 lamb shanks, deboned,
or 400g shoulder of lamb
(keeping the bones)
4 potatoes
3 tomatoes
3 courgettes
100g green peas, shelled, or
green beans
3 onions
3 carrots
2 garlic cloves
2 celery sticks
2 bay leaves
2 tablespoons vegetable oil
Salt

1. Dice the meat and place in a saucepan with the bones, a whole, peeled onion, the bay leaves and enough water to cover.
2. Bring to the boil, then turn down the heat and simmer for 1 hour, regularly skimming off any froth.
3. Chop the two remaining onions. Peel and crush the garlic. Peel the celery sticks and chop finely. Cut the courgettes into half-moons, by halving them lengthways and then slicing. Peel the carrots, slicing diagonally. Peel the tomatoes and cut into eight pieces. Peel and dice the potatoes.
4. In a large casserole, sweat the onion and garlic in 2 tablespoons oil until they are transparent.
5. Add the celery, then the carrots. 1 minute later add the courgettes and the green peas or green beans. Sauté for 2 minutes.
6. Add the tomatoes and the lamb's cooking liquid, just enough to cover.
7. Cover, bring to the boil, add the potatoes.
8. Simmer for 10–15 minutes.
9. Add the meat. Season with salt and serve.

Kibbeh

A dish that is fundamental to Lebanese cooking, *kibbeh* is made of a solid mixture of bulgur wheat (see p. 160) and a second ingredient, which is usually meat but can be fish or even a vegetable like pumpkin or potato. *Kibbeh* can be eaten raw, fried, grilled or oven-baked, in the form of small stuffed balls or pancakes, sometimes accompanied by a sauce. Depending on the recipe, they can be served as an appetizer, starter or main course. Meat *kibbeh* are the most popular. The meat is often shoulder of lamb, with the bones and fat removed, but beef rump steak can also be used. Traditionally, the meat was crushed with a stone mortar, with ice to keep it cool, then kneaded by hand with the bulgur wheat. Unless you have a pestle and mortar that are up to the job, you can ask your butcher to put the meat through the mincer twice.

POTATO KIBBEH

PREPARATION: 40 MINS

COOLING: 1 HR

COOKING: 20 MINS

TO MAKE 40 KIBBEH

1kg potatoes (preferably
Charlotte)

200g fine bulgur wheat (see
p. 160)

100g plain white flour

1 onion

1 bunch coriander

1 litre frying oil

Salt

FOR THE SAUCE

250ml yoghurt

2 garlic cloves

2 bunches coriander

Salt

1. Cook the potatoes in boiling salted water for 15 minutes.
2. Peel and crush them while hot, with a fork, then place in the fridge for 1 hour.
3. Peel the onion. Blend the onion, the bunch of coriander and 100g of the bulgur wheat in a food processor.
4. Place the potato mash, the remaining bulgur and the flour in a large bowl along with the blended onion-coriander-bulgur mixture and add salt.
5. Mash with a fork or pestle until you have an even paste.
6. Shape the paste into small balls 3cm in diameter, flatten and fry in hot oil.

SAUCE

7. Peel the garlic. Combine the coriander, garlic and salt in a food processor. When it is finely minced, add half the yoghurt, blend again, then incorporate the rest of the yoghurt without blending.
8. Serve the *kibbeh* hot, with the sauce.

VARIATIONS

- You can also cook potato *kibbeh* in the oven: instead of shaping into balls, spread a layer of the paste 2cm thick in an ovenproof dish, trickle olive oil on top and place in a 180°C oven (gas mark 6) for 12 minutes.
- You can omit the flour from this recipe. If you do, it's not necessary to cook the mixture in the oven; drizzle the olive oil on top and eat cold.

COMMENT

- You can serve *kibbeh* with two other sauces: the orange pumpkin sauce of Pumpkin Kibbeh (see p. 62) and the red beetroot sauce of Kibbeh Meshwiyeh (see p. 64).

PUMPKIN KIBBEH

PREPARATION: 1HR 30 MINS

COOLING: 1HR

COOKING: 1HR 30 MINS

TO MAKE 40 KIBBEH

2kg pumpkin flesh
100g Charlotte potatoes
200g fine bulgur wheat (see p. 160)
100g plain white flour
1 litre frying oil
Salt

FOR THE STUFFING

1kg onions
50g shelled nuts
2 tablespoons *debs remmane* (pomegranate molasses see p. 166)
50ml vegetable oil

FOR THE SAUCE

100g cooked pumpkin (from making the kibbeh – see step 4)
250ml yoghurt
1 garlic clove
1 teaspoon dried mint
Salt

KIBBEH

1. Peel the potatoes. Cut the pumpkin into large quarters and cook in water for 20 minutes with the potatoes.
2. Strain in a sieve over a container, pressing to extract the most water possible.
3. Reserve 500ml of the cooking water. Place in the fridge.
4. Set aside 100g pumpkin for the sauce.
5. In a food processor, reduce the pumpkin to a purée and then the potato, separately. Then mix them together.
6. Add the bulgur wheat, the flour and salt and stir until you have a smooth paste.
7. Keep in the fridge for 1 hour, uncovered, to allow the bulgur to swell.

STUFFING

8. Peel the onions, chop and sauté in the oil on a low heat, covered, without letting them colour, for 1 hour, stirring from time to time.
9. Coarsely chop the nuts and add them to the onions along with the *debs remmane*.
10. Take the *kibbeh* mixture out of the refrigerator. It should be firm; if not add a handful of bulgur wheat.

MEATBALLS

11. Moisten your hands regularly with the pumpkin's cooking water and shape the mixture into a little pot in the palm of your hand. Fill with the onion and nut mixture, and seal by flattening the edges over the top.
12. Fry in hot oil for around 6 minutes, until golden and crispy.

SAUCE

13. Peel the garlic and crush. Mash the reserved pumpkin with a fork and stir in the yoghurt. Add the garlic, mint and salt. Mix well and serve separately with the meatballs.

VARIATION

- In northern Lebanon, this *kibbeh* is served in an ovenproof dish. The mixture is not fried but spread in two superimposed layers, separated by the stuffing, to which are added 3 Swiss chard leaves, finely chopped. Sesame seeds are scattered over the top with a drizzle of oil, then the *kibbeh* is cooked in the oven at 200°C (gas mark 6–7).

FRIED KIBBEH BALLS

PREPARATION: 1 HR 5 MINS

SOAKING: 10 MINS

COOKING: 35–40 MINS

TO MAKE 40 MEATBALLS

500g minced lamb or rump steak

350g fine bulgur wheat (see p. 160)

1 litre frying oil

Salt and pepper

FOR THE STUFFING

200g minced lamb

6 onions

50g pine nuts (see p. 163)

Salt and pepper

1. Allow the bulgur wheat to soak in cold water for 10 minutes then press with your hands to drain off excess water.

STUFFING

2. Peel and finely chop the onions.
3. Heat 100ml oil in a pan. Sauté the pine nuts until they turn golden, stirring continually and making sure not to burn them.
4. Add the onions and sweat for 15 minutes over a low heat.
5. Add the minced meat, season with salt and pepper, then simmer, uncovered, for 10 minutes.
6. Leave to cool in a sieve.

KIBBEH

7. Meanwhile, thoroughly blend all the ingredients for the *kibbeh* paste, by hand or in a food processor, for 10 minutes – meat, bulgur wheat, salt and pepper. If you are using a food processor, add 3 ice cubes to prevent the paste heating up.
8. Divide the mixture into 35 to 40 small balls. Keep a bowl of iced water close by to wet your fingers, thus ensuring the meatballs remain moist.
9. Take each ball and make a hollow in it with your index finger. Fill with the stuffing and seal (see step-by-step illustrations below).
10. When you have filled every ball, heat the oil in a pan and fry the meatballs for 3 minutes. Serve.

KARIM'S TWIST

Replace the lamb in the filling with currants, walnuts, pistachios and cashews. Add 2 tablespoons honey towards the end of cooking.

Serve with a sauce made of basil, pine nuts (see p. 163) and honey mixed together.

KIBBEH MESHWIYEH

Traditionally, this speciality from the north of Lebanon takes the form of large balls as big as your hand, grilled over a charcoal fire. To make the recipe easier, make smaller balls and grill in the oven.

PREPARATION: 1HR 5 MINS

SOAKING: 10 MINS

COOKING: 6 MINS

TO MAKE 40 MEATBALLS

FOR THE PASTE

500g lean minced lamb, or
minced rump steak
350g fine bulgur wheat (see
p. 160)
Salt and pepper

FOR THE FILLING

1 onion
50g shelled walnuts
1 tablespoon *sumac*
(see p. 162)
1 pinch chilli pepper or a dash
of Tabasco
400g lamb fat (or butter)
Salt

FOR THE SAUCE

250ml yoghurt
1 cooked beetroot
1 garlic clove
1 teaspoon dried mint
Salt

KIBBEH

1. Soak the bulgur wheat in cold water for 10 minutes, sieve and press with your hands to drain off excess water.
2. Mix the bulgur wheat, meat, salt and pepper and stir thoroughly by hand or in a blender for at least 10 minutes. If you use a blender, add 3 ice cubes to prevent the mixture heating up.
3. Put the mixture in the fridge.

STUFFING

4. Peel and chop the onion.
5. Coarsely grind the nuts.
6. Combine the onion, nuts, *sumac*, salt, chilli and the fat you have chosen.
7. Place in the fridge.

MEATBALLS

8. Preheat oven to 210°C (gas mark 7).
9. Take the *kibbeh* and the stuffing out of the fridge, shape into open pots in the palm of your hand, 5cm in diameter, and fill in the same way as for fried *kibbeh* (see p. 63), placing some stuffing into each *kibbeh* and sealing the edges carefully. Place on a tray in the oven.
10. Cook in a hot oven for 6 minutes.

SAUCE

11. Grate the beetroot, peel the garlic clove and crush, or feed through the garlic press with the blade of a knife.
12. Add yoghurt, salt and mint and mix until you have a smooth sauce.

Eat *kibbeh* hot, with the sauce cold or at room temperature. If the *kibbeh* is allowed to cool down, the stuffing will congeal and lose its flavour.

KIBBEH NAYYEH

TARTARE OF KIBBEH

PREPARATION: 15 MINS

SOAKING: 30 MINS

SERVES 6

500g minced lamb or rump
steak
200g fine bulgur wheat (see
p. 160)
50g spring onions
1 bunch mint
A drizzle of fruit-infused olive
oil
20g pine nuts (see p. 163)
Salt and pepper

FOR THE GARNISH

1 bunch mint
1 bunch flat-leaf parsley
10 spring onions
10 cherry tomatoes
1 tablespoon *sumac* (see p.
162)
A drizzle of olive oil

KIBBEH

1. Put the bulgur wheat to soak in a bowl of iced water for 30 minutes.
2. Peel the onions and finely chop. Finely shred the mint and set aside.
3. Place the bulgur wheat in a sieve and press out the excess water. Reserve.
4. Place the meat on a chopping board, add the bulgur, mint and chopped onion, salt and pepper, and knead the mixture by hand.
5. Dip your hands in cold water and knead the mixture again, gradually adding iced water, if necessary, until it is smooth and even.
6. Place the mixture on a dish, sprinkle pine nuts over it and drizzle with olive oil.
7. Eat with pitta bread (see p. 161) and spring onions.

GARNISH

8. Roughly chop the ingredients for the garnish: mint, parsley, tomatoes and spring onions. Sprinkle with *sumac*, drizzle with olive oil and serve separately.
9. This garnish can accompany many different dishes (eg. Falafel see p. 36, grilled meats etc.)

VARIATIONS

- In Lebanon, every region, every family and indeed everyone who loves food has their own recipe for *kibbeh nayyeh*. Some like to use much less bulgur wheat, others increase spices and condiments – chopped basil leaves, cumin, chilli powder etc. – and others still are happy with just a dash of olive oil and nothing more.
- In some of the mountain villages, marjoram is mixed with the meat and *kibbeh* tartare is served with lamb confit. In the north of the country, some of the bulgur wheat is replaced by crushed walnuts. In the south, the meat is not combined with the bulgur wheat but is minced, reduced to a purée with salt and served with *kammouneh* (a mixture of bulgur wheat and onion, mint, cumin, basil, marjoram and dried rose petals).

FISH KIBBEH

This dish is usually made with Mediterranean bass (sea bass). You can also use a mixture of pollack and monkfish. Serve with Tajine Sauce.

PREPARATION: 30 MINS

COOKING: 20 MINS

SERVES 6

300g pollack or cod fillets

300g monkfish

300g fine bulgur wheat (see p. 160)

100g plain white flour

3 onions

2 bunches coriander

1 orange (unwaxed)

50g pine nuts (see p. 163)

1g saffron powder

100ml oil

Salt and pepper

To accompany
Tajine Sauce (p. 29)

1. Preheat the oven to 200°C (gas mark 6–7).
2. Peel and slice 2 onions into rings, sweat for a few minutes in a little oil with the pine nuts, salt and pepper. Add the saffron and arrange in an ovenproof dish.
3. Blend the fish in a food processor until you have a purée.
4. Peel the remaining onion. Grate the orange zest. Separately blend the onion, coriander and orange zest with a handful of bulgur wheat. Add the fish flesh, the rest of the bulgur and the flour, salt and pepper, then knead by hand.
5. Spread a layer of the mixture 2cm thick on top of the onions.
6. Make a hole in the middle.
7. Pour in the remaining oil and place in the oven to cook for 15 minutes.
8. Remove the excess oil, leave to cool, and cut into slices.
9. Serve with Tajine Sauce (see p. 29).

VARIATION

- *Fish balls with coriander.* Prepare the mixture without the onions in saffron. Flatten into pancakes and fry in hot oil. Serve as an appetizer.

KIBBEH BIL-SAYNIEH

OVEN-BAKED KIBBEH

PREPARATION: 35 MINS

SOAKING: 30 MINS

COOKING: 1HR

SERVES 6

FOR THE KIBBEH

500g minced lamb or rump steak

350g fine bulgur wheat (see p. 160)

A drizzle of vegetable oil

Salt and pepper

FOR THE FILLING

200g minced lamb

6 onions

50g pine nuts (see p. 163)

100ml vegetable oil

Salt and pepper

1. Soak the bulgur wheat in cold water for 10 minutes, sieve and press with your hands to drain off excess water.

FILLING

2. Peel and chop the onions; set aside.
3. Pour 100ml oil into a frying pan and sauté the pine nuts until they are golden, stirring continually to avoid burning.
4. Add the onions and sweat for 15 minutes on a low heat.
5. Add the minced meat, salt and pepper, and simmer for about 10 minutes, uncovered.
6. Leave to cool in a sieve.

PASTE

7. Meanwhile, thoroughly combine the meat, bulgur, salt and pepper by hand or in a food processor for at least 10 minutes. If you use a food processor, add 3 ice cubes to prevent the mixture warming up.

MAKING THE KIBBEH

8. Preheat the oven to 200°C (gas mark 6–7).
9. Coat an ovenproof dish with oil and spread half the paste over it, pressing it down with your fingers. Cover with the filling, then spread the other half of the paste on top of the filling to completely cover. Make a hole in the middle with your finger.
10. Decorate the top with the tip of a knife, tracing horizontal and vertical lines. Drizzle oil all over and cook in the oven for 20 minutes.
11. Remove from the oven, drain off the excess oil and cut into slices.
12. Eat with a cabbage or lettuce salad, a tomato salad, or Yoghurt with Cucumber (see facing page).

VARIATION

- Some people serve *kibbeh* hot, covered with 2 tablespoons of cold yoghurt.

KIBBEH WITH YOGHURT

PREPARATION: 60 MINS

COOKING: 30 MINS

TO MAKE 40 KIBBEH

40 fried *kibbeh* balls (see p. 63)
1.5 kg yoghurt
15g corn flour
100g short-grain rice
2 garlic cloves
1 bunch coriander
1 tablespoon vegetable oil

1. Prepare the fried *kibbeh* balls following the recipe on p. 63.

SAUCE

2. Rinse the rice. Cook for 20 minutes in 250ml boiling water.
3. Peel the garlic. Mix the corn flour with the yoghurt.
4. Bring the yoghurt to the boil in a heavy-bottomed saucepan, whisking regularly. Add the rice with its cooking water.
5. Add the *kibbeh* balls and the crushed garlic.
6. Cook for another 10 mins on a low heat, then leave to cool.
7. Wash the coriander. Finely shred then sauté in a little oil.
8. Serve the yoghurt *kibbeh* cold, sprinkled with the sautéed coriander.

VARIATIONS

- In the Bekaa plain, tarragon is used instead of coriander.
- This dish can also be served hot with Basmati Rice (see p. 77). In this case the recipe is identical but rice is omitted.

KHIAR BI LABAN

YOGHURT WITH CUCUMBER

The ideal accompaniment for Kibbeh Bil-Saynieh.

PREPARATION: 10 MINS

SERVES 6

1 litre yoghurt
3 small cucumbers or 1 large cucumber
1 garlic clove
1 tablespoon dried mint
Salt

1. Cut the cucumbers into semi-circles by halving them lengthways and slicing, without peeling or de-seeding. Peel and crush the garlic.
2. Pour the yoghurt into a salad bowl, combine with the cucumber, the crushed garlic and salt, mix well and refrigerate until serving.
3. Just before serving, sprinkle with dried mint.

Vegetable Dishes

YAKHNET-BEMIEH

GREEK HORN OR OKRA RAGOUT

The word yakhne, *borrowed from the Turkish, refers to a category of traditional family dishes, consisting of a green vegetable or pulse, onions, various spices and a little lamb, accompanied by white rice or rice with vermicelli. Similar to stew, this recipe can take many forms, depending on the season, personal taste or budget. Although the basic principle has remained the same for centuries, it goes without saying that the elements have evolved; for example, today we include much more meat than in Ottoman times. But a vegetarian* yakhne *is perfectly possible.*

PREPARATION: 25 MINS

COOKING: 30 MINS

SERVES 6

400g shoulder of lamb, bones
and fat removed

1kg small okra (fresh or
frozen)

20 pearl onions

3 ripe tomatoes

2 bunches coriander

1 whole bulb of garlic

Juice of 1 lemon

500ml water or chicken stock

Vegetable oil

Salt and pepper

1. Chop the meat into 2cm cubes. In a large casserole, sear in a little oil and reserve.
2. If the okra are fresh, cut away the conical cap from the stalk end with a knife. Take care not to pierce the okra themselves or they will turn sticky. If the okra are frozen, use as they are.
3. Fry the okra in a little oil and reserve.
4. Peel the pearl onions and the garlic and chop the coriander. Blanch, peel, de-seed the tomatoes and cut into quarters.
5. Heat some oil in the large casserole and sauté the onions for a few minutes, add the okra, lamb, tomatoes, coriander and all the garlic cloves, whole. Cover with water or chicken stock, add salt and pepper, bring to the boil and then simmer, covered, for 20 minutes.
6. Add the lemon juice and serve with Rice with Vermicelli (see p. 77).

VARIATION

- Towards the end of cooking, you can add 1 clove of garlic, crushed, with a few snips of fresh mint.

GOOD TO KNOW

You can find frozen okra in Middle-Eastern food shops.

YAKHNET-ARDICHAWKEH

RAGOUT OF ARTICHOKE HEARTS

PREPARATION: 10 MINS

COOKING: 30 MINS

SERVES 6

400g shoulder of lamb, bones
and fat removed

12 artichoke hearts (fresh or
frozen)

12 new potatoes

18 pearl onions

Juice of ½ a lemon

1 tablespoon plain white
flour

500ml water or chicken stock

Vegetable oil

Salt and black pepper

1. Chop the meat into 3cm cubes. In a large casserole, sear in a little oil and reserve.
2. Peel the potatoes and deep-fry for 2 to 3 minutes.
3. Without defrosting first if frozen, place the artichoke hearts, potatoes and onions in the large casserole with the meat, cover with water or chicken stock, adding salt and pepper.
4. Bring to the boil and then simmer, covered, for 20 minutes.
5. Add the flour, mixed with a little water, stir and cook for another 5 minutes. Add the lemon juice after removing from the heat.
6. Serve with rice or Rice with Vermicelli (see p. 77).

YAKHNET-BAZELLAH

PEA RAGOUT

PREPARATION: 30 MINS

COOKING: 30 MINS

SERVES 6

400g shoulder of lamb, bones
and fat removed

2kg fresh green peas

3 carrots

1 bunch coriander

2 onions

2 garlic cloves

2 tomatoes or 150ml tomato
juice

500ml water or chicken stock

Vegetable oil

Salt and black pepper

1. Chop the meat into 2cm cubes. In a large casserole, sear in a little oil. Remove from the casserole and set aside.
2. Shell the peas; peel and chop the carrots diagonally. Peel the onions and finely chop. Peel and crush the garlic and finely shred the coriander. Peel the tomatoes, de-seed and cut into pieces.
3. In the large casserole, sauté the onions in a little oil until golden, add the coriander and garlic, then the carrots and peas and finally the lamb and tomatoes.
4. Cover with water or chicken stock, season with salt and pepper and bring to the boil. Simmer on a low heat for 20 minutes.
5. Serve with white rice or Rice with Vermicelli (see p. 77)

YAKHNET-BATATA

POTATO RAGOUT

PREPARATION: 15 MINS

COOKING: 30 MINS

SERVES 6

400g shoulder of lamb,
deboned

1kg Charlotte potatoes

4 very ripe large tomatoes

2 onions

2 garlic cloves

2 bunches coriander

200ml water or chicken stock

Vegetable oil

Salt and pepper

1. Peel the potatoes and cut each into two or three chunks.
2. Chop the lamb shoulder into 3cm cubes. Peel and chop the onions. Peel and crush the garlic cloves. Finely shred the coriander.
3. Peel the tomatoes, de-seed and cut into eight pieces.
4. In a large casserole, sear the lamb on all sides in a little oil. Remove and set aside.
5. In the large casserole, sauté the onion in a little oil.
6. Add the coriander and then the potatoes.
7. Add the lamb, tomatoes, water or chicken stock, salt and pepper.
8. Cover and simmer for 20 minutes.
9. Serve with Basmati Rice or Rice with Vermicelli (see facing page).

YAKHNET-LOUBIEH

GREEN BEAN RAGOUT

PREPARATION: 15 MINS

COOKING: 30 MINS

SERVES 6

400g shoulder of lamb, deboned

1kg green beans, preferably runner beans

2 onions

1 bunch coriander

2 tomatoes or 150ml tomato juice

2 garlic cloves

4 tablespoons vegetable oil

500ml water or chicken stock

Salt and pepper

1. Chop the shoulder of lamb into 3cm cubes.
2. Wash the beans and cut into 3 pieces, diagonally.
3. Peel the tomatoes, de-seed and cut into eight pieces.
4. Peel and chop the onions.
5. Peel and crush the garlic, finely shred the coriander.
6. In a large casserole, brown the lamb for 2 minutes in 2 tablespoons of oil; remove lamb and reserve.
7. In the large casserole, sauté the onions in 2 tablespoons of oil until golden, add the beans and sauté for 5 minutes.
8. Add the lamb, tomato, garlic, coriander, salt and pepper, cover with water or chicken stock and leave to simmer, covered, for 20 minutes.
9. Serve with Basmati Rice or Rice with Vermicelli (see below).

BASMATI RICE

PREPARATION: 5 MINS

COOKING: 25 MINS

SERVES 6

400g basmati rice

2 tablespoons vegetable oil

Salt

1. Thoroughly rinse the rice until the rinsing water runs completely transparent. Do not soak.
2. Sauté the rice in the oil until it is translucent.
3. Add 700ml water and salt. Cover and bring to the boil.
4. Simmer very gently for about 15 minutes until the water is absorbed. Remove from the heat.
5. Leave the rice covered for 10 minutes before serving.

RICE WITH VERMICELLI

PREPARATION: 5 MINS

COOKING: 20 MINS

SERVES 6

400g long-grain rice

100g vermicelli

3 tablespoons vegetable oil

Salt

1. Fry the vermicelli in the oil until golden, add the long-grain rice, sauté.
2. Add salt, cover, and bring to the boil.
3. Simmer very gently until the water is absorbed.
4. Remove from the heat, leaving the rice covered for 10 minutes before serving.

YAKHNET-FASSOULIAH

WHITE BEAN RAGOUT

PREPARATION: 25 MINS

COOKING: 50 MINS

SERVES 6

400g shoulder of lamb, fat
and bones removed
600g fresh white haricot
beans or 400g dried white
haricot beans
2 bunches coriander
2 onions
2 garlic cloves
150ml tomato juice
2 tablespoons olive oil
500ml water or chicken stock
Salt and black pepper

THE DAY BEFORE

1. If you have chosen dried haricot beans, soak them in plenty of cold water. If they are fresh, do not soak, simply blanch on the day.

ON THE DAY

2. Drain the beans and blanch (place in cold water and bring to the boil). Drain again.
3. Cook for 20 minutes in the water and drain again.
4. Chop the shoulder of lamb into 2cm cubes. Peel and chop the onions, finely shred the coriander. Peel and crush the garlic.
5. In a large casserole, brown the lamb in the oil, add the chopped onion until it turns golden then add the garlic and coriander, the beans and the tomato juice.
6. Add salt and pepper, cover with water or chicken stock and bring to the boil.
7. Cover and simmer on a low heat for 20 minutes.
8. Serve with rice or Rice with Vermicelli (see p. 77)

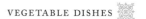

FATTEH

Fatteh *comes from the word* fatt, *already mentioned in connection with* fattoush, *which relates to the action of crumbling. It refers to the many different yoghurt-based dishes that contain broken pieces of bread. These recipes probably originated with the desire to use up leftover bread, which was no longer fresh but which we could not throw away, and so incorporated into a salad, main course or a dessert. These days we're more likely to fry or grill the bread. Here are four* fatteh *recipes, two 'classics' (one with chickpeas, one with aubergines), one 'forgotten' vegetable* fatteh *that was passed down to Karim from his grandmother, and one modern* fatteh *with asparagus, which Karim invented. The bread was traditionally laid at the bottom of the dish, but that way it goes soft and loses its crispiness, so it's better to place it on top, with pine nuts. If, on the other hand, you would rather avoid frying, you can grill the bread in the oven at 150ºC (gas mark 5) for around 20 minutes.*

The yoghurt can be served hot or cold, depending on the recipe or the season.

AUBERGINE FATTEH

PREPARATION: 20 MINS

RESTING: 1 NIGHT

COOKING: 15 MINS

SERVES 6

12 mini aubergines or 3 large ones

300g minced lamb

2 tomatoes

1 onion

6 basil leaves

4 garlic cloves

2 pitta bread

50g pine nuts (see p. 163)

500ml yoghurt

2 tablespoons red wine vinegar

2 tablespoons *tahini* (sesame paste, see p. 167)

Vegetable oil

Salt and pepper

THE DAY BEFORE

1. Peel the aubergines. If they are large, cut them in half lengthways and then into quarters.
2. Sprinkle with salt, place in a colander and leave to drain in the fridge.

ON THE DAY

3. Fry the aubergines in oil, pat them dry with kitchen paper and keep somewhere warm.
4. Peel the garlic cloves and the onion. Chop 2 of the garlic cloves, the onion, tomatoes and basil and sauté them all in a pan with a little oil.
5. Add the lamb and cook on a high flame, uncovered, for 5 minutes. Add salt and pepper.
6. Season the yoghurt with the remaining 2 garlic cloves, crushed, and with vinegar, *tahini* and salt.
7. Cut the bread into small squares, fry (or grill in the oven) and reserve.
8. In a deep serving bowl, arrange the aubergines, lamb and yoghurt, and scatter with the squares of fried bread and dry-roasted golden pine nuts.

VARIATION

- You may prefer the flavours to melt together. If so, cook the aubergines a second time, covered, with the minced meat and a little water, over a low heat, for 10 minutes.

FATTET-HALIOUN, WITH ASPARAGUS

PREPARATION: 20 MINS

COOKING: 30 MINS

SERVES 6

4 bundles asparagus
4 garlic cloves
500ml yoghurt
2 pitta bread (see p. 161)
1 teaspoon corn flour
50g pine nuts (see p. 163)
3 tablespoons vegetable oil
Salt and pepper

1. Trim the asparagus and immerse in a saucepan full of cold water. Turn up the heat and as soon as the water boils, remove the asparagus. Cut off the asparagus stems, leaving two-thirds, with the heads. Set aside.
2. Cook the asparagus stems in salted boiling water for ten minutes. Blend in a food processor with a little of the cooking water.
3. Add the yoghurt to the corn flour, place in a heavy-bottomed pan and bring to the boil.
4. Stir in the blended asparagus and bring to the boil. Reserve.
5. Peel the garlic, and finely chop. Briefly sauté with the asparagus heads in 2 tablespoons oil. Add salt and pepper.
6. Cut the bread into small squares or strips, fry (or oven bake) and reserve.
7. Fry the pine nuts in 1 tablespoon oil until golden.
8. In a deep serving bowl, arrange the asparagus heads in a fan with the hot yoghurt, bread and pine nuts on top. Serve.

FATTET-HUMMUS, WITH CHICKPEAS

PREPARATION: 15 MINS

SOAKING: 1 NIGHT

COOKING: 45 MINS

SERVES 6

300g chickpeas
2 pitta bread (see p. 161)
50g pine nuts (see p. 163)
500ml yoghurt
1 tablespoon red wine vinegar
1 garlic clove
2 tablespoons *tahini* (sesame paste, see p. 167)
A few sprigs of flat-leaf parsley (optional)
Vegetable oil
Salt

THE DAY BEFORE

1. Soak the chickpeas in 2 litres of water.

ON THE DAY

2. Rinse the chickpeas in water and cook in a large casserole in 2 litres of water, on a low heat, for 45 minutes.
3. Add salt and set aside somewhere warm.
4. Fry the pine nuts in a little oil until golden.
5. Slice the bread into small squares, fry (or oven bake) and reserve.
6. Peel and crush the garlic. Combine with the yoghurt, vinegar, *tahini* and salt.
7. Ladle the chickpeas and a little of their cooking water into each bowl, cover with 3 tablespoons yoghurt, sprinkle with the squares of fried bread and pine nuts, and top with a little chopped parsley. Serve.

FATTET-KHODRA, WITH VEGETABLES

PREPARATION: 30 MINS

COOKING: 25–30 MINS

SERVES 6

2 onions

4 garlic cloves

3 courgettes

3 carrots

2 sticks celery

4 potatoes (preferably Charlotte)

3 tomatoes

100g shelled green peas or 100g green beans

500ml yoghurt

2 tablespoons red wine vinegar

2 tablespoons *tahini* (sesame paste, see p. 167)

2 pitta bread (see p. 161)

50g pine nuts (see p. 163)

Vegetable oil

Salt and pepper

1. Peel and chop the onions.
2. Peel the garlic. Crush 2 garlic cloves and set aside the other 2.
3. Peel and finely chop the celery sticks.
4. Peel the carrots, cut in half lengthways and then diagonally.
5. Cut the courgettes in half lengthways and slice.
6. Peel and de-seed the tomatoes then cut into eight pieces.
7. Peel the potatoes and cut into small cubes.
8. In a large casserole, fry the onions lightly in 2 tablespoons oil until transparent, then add the crushed garlic.
9. Add the celery, then the carrots, add the courgettes 1 minute later and then the peas or beans and sauté for 2 minutes.
10. Add the tomatoes and then water to fill two-thirds of the casserole; add salt and pepper. Cover and bring to the boil.
11. Add the potatoes and simmer for 10–15 minutes, covered.
12. Cut the bread into small squares, fry (or oven bake) and reserve.
13. Fry the pine nuts in a little oil.
14. Season the yoghurt with the two remaining garlic cloves, crushed, and the vinegar, *tahini* and salt.
15. Arrange the vegetables in a serving bowl and pour a little of the cooking liquid over them. Add the yoghurt and sprinkle with fried or grilled bread and pine nuts. Serve.

AUBERGINES WITH EWE'S MILK YOGHURT

PREPARATION: 10 MINS

COOKING: 35 MINS

RESTING: 1 NIGHT

SERVES 6

4 aubergines

1kg ewe's milk yoghurt

300g minced lamb

50g pine nuts (see p. 163)

2 tablespoons corn flour

Vegetable oil

Salt and ground black pepper

THE DAY BEFORE

1. Peel the aubergines and cut in two widthways, then each half into four chunks. Sprinkle with plenty of salt and reserve in a colander in the fridge overnight.

ON THE DAY

2. Deep-fry the aubergines for 4 minutes then place on kitchen paper.
3. Put the aubergines in a saucepan and fill with water to cover. Place an upturned dish on top as a weight and cover. Cook for 15 minutes on a low heat.
4. Drain the aubergines, reserving the cooking water.
5. In a heavy-bottomed saucepan, combine the yoghurt and corn flour. Bring to the boil, whisking regularly.
6. Add the aubergines' cooking water. Leave to cook for a minute or two, then pour this mixture over the aubergines, arranged in a bowl. Leave to cool.
7. Fry the pine nuts in a little oil, add the minced lamb, season with salt and pepper.
8. Simmer for 10 minutes on a low heat.
9. Serve the meat very hot and the aubergines at room temperature with Basmati Rice (see p. 77).

KOUSSA BIL-LABAN

COURGETTES STUFFED WITH LAMB AND YOGHURT

PREPARATION: 40 MINS

COOKING: 35–40 MINS

SERVES 6

300g minced lamb
18 small courgettes
150g short-grain rice
50ml olive oil
Salt and black pepper

FOR THE YOGHURT SAUCE

1kg yoghurt
2 tablespoons cornflour
1 tablespoon dried mint
2 garlic cloves

1. Top and tail the courgettes, halve, then scoop out the insides with a vegetable peeler and set aside.
2. Rinse the rice and combine with the meat and olive oil. Add salt and pepper.
3. Stuff the courgettes with the rice and meat mixture, pack them tightly in a saucepan, simmer, covered, for 15 minutes with enough salted water to cover.
4. To prepare the sauce: mix the yoghurt and corn flour in a heavy-bottomed saucepan. Bring to the boil, whisking regularly.
5. Peel and crush the garlic. Add to the sauce, with the dried mint.
6. Arrange the courgettes in a large saucepan with the sauce and a little of the courgettes' cooking water, according to taste.
7. Simmer for a further 10 minutes.
8. Serve hot, garnished with fresh mint leaves.

ABLAMA

SELECTION OF STUFFED VEGETABLES

PREPARATION: 45 MINS

COOKING: 25 MINS

SERVES 6

6 round courgettes

6 medium-sized potatoes

10 medium-sized tomatoes

500g minced lamb

50g pine nuts (see p. 163)

4 onions

Juice of 1 lemon

500ml chicken stock

Vegetable oil

Salt and pepper

TO ACCOMPANY

Greek-style yoghurt

1. Cut the top third off the courgettes, 6 tomatoes and the peeled potatoes, making lids. Scoop out the insides and set aside.
2. Reserve the tomato pulp.
3. Fry the potato and courgette flesh you have scooped out for 3 minutes. Set aside.
4. Chop the onions.
5. Fry the pine nuts in a little oil; add half the onions and sauté for 3 minutes.
6. Add the minced meat, salt and pepper, and cook for a further 2 minutes.
7. Stuff the vegetables with this mixture and replace the lids.
8. Sauté the remaining onions in a saucepan with a little oil; arrange on top of the stuffed vegetables.
9. Peel the remaining tomatoes, cut into eight pieces and combine with the tomato pulp and the lemon juice. Pour the tomato mixture over the vegetables in the saucepan. Add as much stock as you need to cover the vegetables and simmer for 20 minutes, covered.
10. Serve with Basmati Rice or Rice with Vermicelli (see p. 77).
11. Stir the yoghurt, add a pinch of salt and serve separately.

VARIATION

- You can add other vegetables such as red peppers or aubergines, and prepare in the same way as the courgettes.

STUFFED CABBAGE LEAVES

PREPARATION: 45 MINS

COOKING: 30 MINS

SERVES 6

1 green cabbage
500g minced lamb
150g short-grain rice
2 whole bulbs garlic
1 bunch mint or 15g dried mint
200ml lemon juice
500ml water or chicken stock
Salt and black pepper

1. Plunge the cabbage into boiling water for 3 minutes then take out and allow to cool. Separate the leaves, drying carefully, then remove the stalks.
2. Rinse the rice.
3. Combine the rice with the meat, adding salt and pepper.
4. Lay the cabbage leaves on your work surface. Place a little stuffing (rice and meat) in each one and roll it over, pressing hard. Repeat until you have used up the mixture.
5. Place a quarter of the cut cabbage stalks and the whole, unpeeled garlic cloves in a saucepan, setting aside 2 of them.
6. Place the stuffed cabbage leaves on top, packing tightly.
7. Cover with water or chicken stock. Simmer, covered, for 20 minutes.
8. Crush the remaining garlic cloves with the mint. Add them to the saucepan along with the lemon juice. Briefly bring back to the boil and serve.

SHEIKH EL-MEHSHI

STUFFED AUBERGINES

PREPARATION: 45 MINS

COOKING: 45 MINS

SERVES 6

6 small aubergines
500g minced lamb
2 onions
50g pine nuts (see p. 163)
Vegetable oil
Salt and pepper

FOR THE SAUCE

1 onion
2 garlic cloves
1 stick celery
5 very ripe tomatoes
Olive oil
Salt and black pepper

AUBERGINES

1. Peel and chop the onions.
2. Sauté the pine nuts in 2 tablespoons oil, add the chopped onions, sauté again and add the minced lamb.
3. Season with salt and pepper and cook for 5 minutes.
4. Partially peel the aubergines (in alternate strips).
5. In a frying pan, sauté the aubergines for a few minutes with oil, to soften.
6. Cut the aubergines in half lengthways, scoop out the insides and stuff with the mixture of meat, onions and pine nuts.

SAUCE

7. Peel the tomatoes then cut into pieces. Peel the garlic and onion.
8. Chop the onion, peel the garlic and finely chop the celery.
9. Fry all the ingredients except the tomatoes in olive oil, and then add the tomatoes. Add salt and pepper and simmer for 10 minutes, covered.
10. Place the stuffed aubergines in a saucepan, cover with sauce and leave to simmer for 20 minutes, covered.
11. Serve with rice (see Basmati Rice p. 77).

STUFFED COURGETTES AND STUFFED VINE LEAVES

PREPARATION: 1HR 15MINS

COOKING: 30 MINS

SERVES 6

50 vine leaves, fresh or from
a jar
12 small courgettes
1 best rib of lamb
400g minced lamb
120g short-grain rice
200ml lemon juice
500ml water or chicken stock
Salt and black pepper

1. Cut the courgettes in half lengthways and scoop out the insides. Wash the vine leaves (or drain if from a jar).
2. Rinse the rice and combine with the minced meat, salt and pepper.
3. Stuff the courgettes and the vine leaves with this mixture (see step-by-step illustrations below).
4. Cut the rib into 6.
5. Sear the ribs on each side in a pan. Place in a saucepan.
6. Place the courgettes and vine leaves on top.
7. Cover with water or chicken stock and lemon juice.
8. Place an upturned plate on top for weight, cover and simmer for 20 minutes (more if the vine leaves are from a jar).
9. Turn out on to a plate and serve with a bowl of natural yoghurt.

GOOD TO KNOW

- You can find vine leaves in Middle-Eastern food shops.

MEAT AND POULTRY DISHES

KAFTAHS

KAFTAHS

The main ingredients of kaftah *are minced meat, parsley and onion. Unlike* kibbeh*, it contains no bulgur wheat. The best cut to use for these recipes is shoulder of lamb.*

OVEN-BAKED KAFTAH

PREPARATION: 30 MINS

COOKING: 35 MINS

SERVES 6

FOR THE MEAT

900g minced lamb
1 bunch flat-leaf parsley
2 small onions
Salt and pepper

FOR THE SAUCE

3 onions
1 red pepper
200ml tomato juice
1 tablespoon *debs remmane*
(pomegranate molasses, see
p. 166)
1 tablespoon olive oil
Salt and pepper

FOR THE KAFTAH DISH

3 large potatoes
3 large ripe tomatoes
Vegetable oil

1. Peel the onions. Finely chop the parsley and the onions.
2. Blend the meat with the parsley, the chopped onions, salt and pepper and place in the fridge.

SAUCE

3. Slice the red pepper into thin strips.
4. Peel and finely chop the onions.
5. In a frying pan, sauté the onions and pepper in olive oil over a low heat, until the onion turns translucent. Add the tomato juice, the *debs remmane* and 200ml water, salt and pepper.
6. Bring to the boil, then reserve.

ASSEMBLING THE DISH

7. Peel the potatoes, slice into discs 5mm thick, and deep-fry for 2 minutes. Pat dry with kitchen paper and reserve.
8. Cut the tomatoes into 5mm thick slices.
9. Preheat the oven to 210ºC (gas mark 7).
10. Divide the *kaftah* into 12 balls, flatten and arrange on a lightly oiled ovenproof dish.
11. Place in the oven and cook for 5 minutes.
12. Remove the dish from the oven, cover the meat with a layer of potatoes followed by the tomato slices.
13. Cover with sauce and replace in the oven for 15 minutes.
14. Serve hot.

KAFTAH NAYYEH

TARTARE OF KAFTAH

PREPARATION: 10 MINS

SERVES 6

900g minced lamb or rump
steak (choose the leanest
meat possible)
1 bunch flat-leaf parsley
2 onions or 6 spring onions
1 drizzle olive oil
Salt and black pepper

1. Peel the onions. Finely chop the parsley and the onions.
2. Blend the meat with the salt, pepper, parsley and onions in a food processor for a few minutes.
3. Place on a plate, drizzle olive oil on top and serve.

VARIATION

- You can also add a teaspoon of 7 Spice Mix (see p. 165), a pinch of chilli pepper and chopped red pepper.

KARIM'S TWIST

Fish kaftah. Replace the meat with raw fish. Combine 500g gilthead bream fillets, roughly chopped, 1 bunch of chives, finely chopped, ½ a bunch chopped dill, salt and pepper. Serve with a trickle of olive oil.

GRILLED KAFTAH

PREPARATION: 15 MINS
COOKING: 8 MINS

SERVES 6

900g shoulder of lamb,
minced
1 bunch flat-leaf parsley
2 small onions
2 tablespoons vegetable oil
Salt and black pepper

1. Peel the onions. Finely chop the parsley and the onions.
2. Blend the meat with the parsley, onions, salt and pepper.
3. Shape the meat into sausages, slide onto a skewer and brush with oil.
4. Grill on a barbecue or under the grill in the oven, making sure to turn the *kaftah* halfway through cooking (after about 4 minutes).
5. Eat with Hummus, Fattoush or Tabbouleh (see pp. 30, 15 and 16).

VARIATION

- You can combine the meat with pine nuts (see p. 163).

FRIED KAFTAH MEATBALLS

PREPARATION: 15 MINS

COOKING: 5 MINS

SERVES 6

900g minced lamb

4 eggs

1 bunch flat-leaf parsley

2 small onions

Frying oil

Salt and black pepper

1. Peel the onions. Finely chop the parsley and onions.
2. Blend the meat with salt, pepper, eggs, parsley and chopped onions.
3. Shape the mixture into a dozen flattened balls.
4. Heat the oil in a frying pan and fry the balls for 2 minutes.
5. Serve hot as a *mezze* or with chips.

GRILLED MEATS

QUAIL WITH SUMAC

PREPARATION: 5 MINS

COOKING: 10 MINS

SERVES 6

6 quail

Olive oil

2 tablespoons *sumac*
(see p. 162)

1 tablespoon unsalted,
shelled pistachios

Salt and black pepper

1. Cut each quail in two lengthways. Coat in olive oil, salt, pepper and half the *sumac*.
2. Grind the pistachios.
3. Cook the quail on a grill – a barbecue or oven grill – turning them over halfway through cooking.
4. Before serving, dust generously with *sumac* and ground pistachios.

LAMB CUTLETS WITH 7 SPICES

PREPARATION: 5 MINS

COOKING: 10 MINS

SERVES 6

12 middle-neck lamb chops

Olive oil

7 Spice Mix (see p. 165)

Salt

1. Coat the chops in olive oil and spices.
2. Grill, turning over midway through cooking.
3. Add salt and serve.

GOOD TO KNOW

- This dish goes very well with a Coral Lentil Moujaddara (see p. 35) and Tomatoes with Cumin (see p. 18).

SHISH TAOUK

Chicken kebabs marinated in 7 Spices. This recipe is Ottoman in origin. In Turkish, shish means stick and taouk means chicken. For the tastiest chicken, cook for as short a time as possible, or it will dry out; also, do not use salt in the marinade.

PREPARATION: 10 MINS

MARINADE: 24 HRS

COOKING: 12 MINS

SERVES 6

900g chicken breast
4 garlic cloves
100ml olive oil
1 teaspoon 7 Spice Mix (see p. 165)
Salt and black pepper

THE DAY BEFORE

1. Chop the chicken breast into 3cm chunks. Peel and crush the garlic.
2. Marinate the chicken for 24 hrs in a mixing bowl with the garlic, olive oil, pepper and 7 Spice Mix, but without salt, which could dry out the chicken.

ON THE DAY

3. Skewer the chunks of chicken on a kebab stick and grill on a barbecue or oven grill. Season with salt.
4. Serve with Cream of Garlic (see below).

VARIATIONS

- Instead of using skewers, place the chunks of chicken in an ovenproof dish and cook for 15 minutes at 180°C (gas mark 6).
- Marinate the chicken chunks with the bones and skin. Cook on a barbecue. The skin will prevent the chicken from drying out. Or, use a whole poussin (baby chicken), with or without bones.
- *Shish taouk* marinade often has more flavours than the one here. If you like, you can add lemon juice, which prevents the meat discolouring; red wine vinegar, which should soften the meat, chilli powder, 1 crushed bay leaf, or even 1 tablespoon tomato purée. Hummus (see p. 30) goes wonderfully with this dish.

TOUM BEZEIT

CREAM OF GARLIC WITH OIL

PREPARATION: 15 MINS

COOLING: 2 HRS

SERVES 6

1 whole bulb garlic
150ml vegetable oil

1. Cool oil in the fridge for 2hrs.
2. Peel the garlic. Place in a food processor and reduce to a fine purée.
3. Take the oil out of the fridge and add to the garlic in a thin trickle to make it stiffen like a mayonnaise.

GOOD TO KNOW

- It is easier to make this cream if you add 1 boiled potato or 1 egg white, unbeaten.
- You can scald the garlic to make it less spicy.

FARROUJ MESHWI

GRILLED CHICKEN WITH GARLIC

PREPARATION: 15 MINS

COOLING: 12 HRS

COOKING: 15 MINS

SERVES 4

2 poussins (baby chickens),
deboned
2 garlic cloves
Juice of ½ a lemon
100ml olive oil
7 Spice Mix (see p. 165)
Salt and pepper

THE DAY BEFORE

1. Peel and crush the garlic. Mix together the garlic, salt, pepper, lemon juice, oil and pour the mixture on to the poussins.
2. Cover and place in the fridge for 12 hrs.
3. Turn the poussins after 6 hrs.

ON THE DAY

4. Put the oven on grill function and preheat your grill for 10 minutes.
5. Remove the poussins from the marinade and place in an ovenproof dish.
6. Cook for 15 minutes, turning over halfway through and at the end of cooking to end with the skin underneath. To produce a grilling effect, leave the oven door ajar.
7. Serve with Cream of Garlic with Oil (see facing page).

LEG OF LAMB WITH RICE AND BROAD BEANS

PREPARATION: 30 MINS

COOKING: 1HR 50 MINS

SERVES 6

1 leg of lamb or, even better, a saddle of suckling lamb
500g fresh tender broad beans, in their pods
1 onion
300g basmati rice
50g pine nuts (see p. 163)
50g whole blanched almonds
50g shelled unsalted whole pistachios
Vegetable oil
1 teaspoon 7 Spice Mix (see p. 165)
Salt and black pepper

1. Peel the onion and cut in half.
2. In a large casserole, heat the oil and sear the leg of lamb on all sides. Cover with water. Season with salt and pepper, add the onion, and simmer, covered, for 1hr 30 mins. Set aside.
3. Cut the broad beans diagonally, in pieces 3cm long. Cook for 20 minutes in salted water, covered, to stop them discolouring. Remove the lid after cooking.
4. In a high-sided frying pan, sauté the rice in 2 tablespoons oil until translucent.
5. Add 250ml of the beans' cooking water and 250ml of the lamb's cooking water.
6. Add the 7 Spice Mix. Bring to the boil, cover and simmer for 7 minutes.
7. Add the strained beans, cover again and cook for another 4 minutes.
8. In a saucepan, bring the almonds and pistachios to the boil for a few minutes in 2 glasses of water, then run under cold water and remove the skins. Cut the almonds in half lengthways.
9. Fry the pine nuts, pistachios and almonds in turn with a little oil until they are golden. Reserve on kitchen paper.
10. Mix the rice and the beans in a serving dish, place the tender lamb on top and sprinkle with pine nuts, almonds and pistachios. Serve.

FIVE SPICE LAMB AND RICE

PREPARATION: 30 MINS

COOKING: 2 HRS 40 MINS

SERVES 6

1 shoulder of lamb
300g basmati rice
1 carrot
3 onions
100ml tomato juice
1 tablespoon whole black
peppercorns
1 tablespoon whole green
cardamoms
1 tablespoon cinnamon
powder
1 tablespoon cloves
1 tablespoon cumin powder
30g raisins
30g pine nuts (see p. 163)
30g whole almonds
30g unsalted shelled
pistachios
Vegetable oil
Salt

1. Ask your butcher to remove the fat from the shoulder of lamb and to chop it into 15 pieces, with bone in each cut.
2. Peel the onions and cut into quarters. Peel the carrot and cut into juliennes (thin batons).
3. Pour 2 tablespoons oil into a pan and sauté the onion on a high flame until golden. Reserve. Sweat the carrot in the same oil and reserve.
4. In a large casserole, sear all sides of the lamb chunks on a high flame. Add the onion, tomato juice and cover with water 2cm above the meat. Add salt. Place the spices in a muslin bag, add to the large casserole, then cover. Bring to the boil, turn down the heat and leave to simmer very gently for 2 hrs.
5. Bring the almonds and pistachios to the boil in a saucepan with 2 glasses of water for a few minutes, then run under cold water and remove the skins. Slice the almonds in half lengthways.
6. Sauté the pine nuts, pistachios and almonds in turn in the oil. Set aside on kitchen paper.
7. When the lamb is cooked, remove and sieve the stock. Reserve 500ml for cooking the rice. Cover the meat with the rest of the cooking juice.
8. Rinse and drain the rice.
9. Heat the oil, add the rice and carrot batons and stir with a wooden spatula until the rice is translucent. This should take around 3 minutes.
10. Add the reserved cooking juice. Bring to the boil, cover and simmer for 10 minutes. Remove from the heat and keep covered.
11. Serve the rice and the meat without the cooking juice, sprinkled with pine nuts, pistachios, almonds and raisins.

GOOD TO KNOW

• You can replace the shoulder of lamb with 3 lamb shanks.

FREEKKET-TOUYOUR WITH THREE BIRDS

PREPARATION: 25 MINS

COOKING: 1HR 40 MINS

SERVES 6

3 quail

3 pigeon

3 partridge

1 leek

1 carrot

1 onion

300g *freekeh* (see p. 168)

2 tablespoons vegetable oil

Salt and black pepper

1. Preheat the oven to 180°C (gas mark 6).
2. Ask your butcher to remove the bones from 1 quail, 1 pigeon and 1 partridge. Keep the scraps and trimmings (skin, fat, nerves, bones etc.).
3. Boil the bones and off-cuts for 30 minutes in 1 litre of water. Sieve, pressing on the bones, and reserve the stock obtained.
4. Chop the raw meat into small cubes. Peel the onion, leek and carrot and cut into small dice, sauté in oil with the meat, add the unrinsed *freekeh* and 900ml of the stock.
5. Add salt and pepper, cover, bring to the boil and then simmer on a very low heat for 1 hour.
6. Roast the remaining partridge and pigeon in an ovenproof dish, lightly oiled, for 10 minutes. Then add the quail and cook for 25 minutes. Season with salt and pepper and serve with the *freekeh* as a garnish.

VARIATION
- When in season, add a few fresh figs: 3 figs finely sliced with the vegetables and 3 more, halved, placed on top of the *freekeh* 10 minutes before the end of cooking.

BULGUR BEDFEEN

PREPARATION: 20 MINS

SOAKING: 1 NIGHT

COOKING: 2 HRS

SERVES 6

3 lamb shanks

400g coarse bulgur wheat (see p. 160)

24 small pearl onions

50g chickpeas

1 cinnamon stick

1 tablespoon caraway seeds

Greek-style yoghurt (approx 1200ml)

Vegetable oil

Mild white pepper

Salt

THE DAY BEFORE

1. Soak the chickpeas in plenty of water.

ON THE DAY

2. Peel the onions. Drain the chickpeas.
3. Sauté the onions in a frying pan with a little oil. Add the meat and then the chickpeas.
4. Cover with 2 litres of water, bring to the boil and remove any scum from the broth several times.
5. Add the cinnamon, salt and pepper then cover and simmer for 1hr 30 mins.
6. Take 500ml of the stock and pour into a casserole dish. Add the bulgur wheat, the lamb shanks, chickpeas, pearl onions and caraway, and simmer for 30 minutes.
7. Serve with yoghurt or sauce taken from the stock and well seasoned.

ROYAL MOULOUKHIEH

Originally Egyptian, mouloukhieh *is a dish whose name indicates it was once eaten at royal tables. The word also refers to a green plant that is used exclusively for this dish in Lebanese cookery. Sometimes called Jew's mallow, bush okra or West African sorrel, it belongs to the corchorus family, which also includes jute. It has a long stalk covered in leaves, which resemble spinach leaves but are coarser.* Mouloukhieh *is traditionally eaten in summer, when the plant grows, although this hot, rich dish would be more appropriate for winter. Luckily, pre-cut, washed and frozen leaves can be bought these days, ready for use in any season.*

PREPARATION: 30 MINS

COOKING: 60 MINS

SERVES 6

500g *mouloukhieh*
1 free-range chicken
300g basmati rice (see p. 77)
2 bunches coriander
3 cloves garlic
1 onion
3 shallots
2 pitta bread (see p. 161)
150ml red wine vinegar
1 pinch bicarbonate of soda
Juice of 2 lemons
Vegetable oil
Salt

1. Wash, dry and cut the *mouloukhieh* leaves into very thin strips.
2. In a casserole dish, sear the chicken on every side. Add salt and the whole onion, cover with water and cook for 50 minutes on a medium heat, uncovered.
3. Finely shred the coriander.
4. Peel and crush the garlic.
5. In a frying pan, sauté the garlic and coriander in oil for 3 minutes.
6. Cut the bread into 2cm squares and place under the grill for 1 minute, keeping a close watch, until golden.
7. Peel and chop the shallots, then place in a bowl with the vinegar.
8. Take the chicken out of the stock, remove the skin and bones. Set aside somewhere warm.
9. Add garlic and coriander to the stock, as well as bicarbonate of soda (to retain the *mouloukhieh*'s beautiful green colour), the lemon juice and then the *mouloukhieh*. The moment it begins to bubble, remove from heat.
10. To serve, place in each deep bowl first rice, then chicken, a large ladle of *mouloukhieh* and finally the shallots in vinegar and grilled bread.

VARIATIONS

- Every family has its own way of cooking *mouloukhieh*. You can serve it with lamb or even rabbit and add more onions to the broth, or even tomatoes.
- The vinegar for the chopped shallots can be replaced with lemon juice.
- If you cannot find *mouloukhieh*, you can use fresh spinach.

SEVEN SPICE CHICKEN AND RICE

PREPARATION: 20–30 MINS

COOKING: 1HR 15 MINS

SERVES 6

1 free-range chicken
300g basmati rice
1 onion
1 tablespoon 7 Spice Mix (see
p. 165)
1 teaspoon whole black
peppercorns
30g pine nuts (see p. 163)
30g whole blanched almonds
30g shelled, unsalted
pistachios
Vegetable oil
Salt

OPTIONAL

500g green peas in their pods
or
200g minced lamb + 1 onion

1. Peel the onion and cut into quarters.
2. Brown the chicken all over in the oil. Add the onion and black pepper. Cover with water, add salt, bring to the boil. Skim off the surface froth. Simmer on a low heat for 45 minutes.
3. Take the chicken from its stock. Leave it to cool, sieve the broth and reserve.
4. In turn, sauté the pine nuts, pistachios and almonds in oil. Reserve on kitchen paper.
5. Remove the chicken's skin and bones, chop the meat into pieces, replace in a saucepan and cover with stock.
6. Rinse and drain the rice.

1ST VERSION

- Shell the peas.
- Sauté the rice in a frying pan with a little oil (use the oil from frying the pine nuts) until it is translucent. Add the peas.
- Pour 600ml of the stock and half the 7 Spice Mix over the rice. Bring to the boil then simmer on a low heat for 10 minutes. Remove from the heat and keep covered.

2ND VERSION

- Peel and thinly slice the onion. Sauté for a few minutes in a little oil. Add the minced meat and cook for a further 2 minutes.
- In a frying pan, sauté the rice in a little oil until it's translucent. Add the onion and the meat.
- Pour 600ml stock on top, as well as the rest of the 7 Spice Mix. Bring to the boil.
- Simmer very gently for 10 minutes. Remove from the heat and keep covered.

Serve the rice with the chunks of chicken on top, dusted with the rest of the spices and sprinkled with almonds, pistachios and pine nuts.

MAQLOUBET-BATENJAN

AUBERGINE LAYER CAKE

PREPARATION: 45 MINS

SWEATING: 1 NIGHT

COOKING: 2 HRS 30 MINS

SERVES 10

500g minced lamb
8 aubergines
3 onions
1 red pepper
500g basmati rice
70g pine nuts (see p. 163)
70g blanched almonds
20g blanched pistachios
Vegetable oil
Salt and black pepper

THE DAY BEFORE

1. Peel the aubergines, cut in half widthways, then cut each half into four, add salt and place in a colander in the fridge.

ON THE DAY

2. In turn, sauté the pine nuts, pistachios and almonds in oil. Set aside on kitchen paper.
3. Fry the aubergines in oil and pat dry with kitchen paper.
4. Place the aubergines in the bottom of a saucepan and cover with water. Place a weight on top, a plate for example (the aubergines should stay at the bottom of the pan). Cover and cook on a low heat for 10 minutes. Drain, reserving the cooking water.
5. Peel the onions. Chop the onions and the pepper, de-seeded, and sauté in 2 tablespoons oil. Add the minced meat, season with salt and pepper and cook for 5 minutes. Rinse the rice.
6. Heat 2 tablespoons oil in a saucepan and sauté the rice until it is translucent. Add the aubergines' cooking water to twice the volume of the rice, adding water if necessary. Bring to the boil, cover and simmer for 7 minutes. Remove from the heat and keep covered.
7. Pour half the rice into a large saucepan, place the aubergines on top, then the meat, then the rest of the rice.
8. Cover with greaseproof paper, put a plate on top as a weight, cover and cook for 1hr 45 mins on a very low heat.
9. Remove the lid, the plate and the greaseproof paper, put a plate over the saucepan and quickly turn over.
10. Gently pull the saucepan upwards, to turn out the cake, and mop up the surplus sauce.
11. Sprinkle with pine nuts, almonds and pistachios.
12. Serve as a cake with the crunchy rice on top.

VARIATIONS

*   You can replace the minced meat with lamb shanks, deboned and chopped into 3cm chunks.
*   Coarse bulgur wheat (see p. 160) can be substituted for rice. Bulgur wheat is easier to cook since it remains firm. The downside is that you won't have the surface of crunchy rice. Lay the aubergines on the bottom of the saucepan so that they will be on top of the cake.

GOOD TO KNOW

*   You can prepare everything in advance; place the ingredients in the saucepan and begin to cook 1hr 45 mins before serving.

LAMB AND WHEAT HRISSEH WITH CINNAMON

This is a festive dish enjoyed by different eastern communities over the centuries, from the Armenians of Constantinople to the Chaldeans of Iraq and Iran. In some Christian villages in the Lebanese mountains, hrisseh *is traditionally prepared for 15th August, the feast of the Virgin. The evening before, a fire is lit in the church square. Chunks of lamb with bones and onions are stewed in a big copper cauldron. In the early morning, the bones are removed from the cauldron, wheat is added and the cooking goes on for several more hours, until mass is over. Plates of* hrisseh *are then offered to the faithful, who eat them there in small groups or take them home for the family meal.*

A similar tradition exists in the Shiite villages and towns of South Lebanon, to celebrate the feast of Achoura. Rich families prepare the hrisseh *in big copper cauldrons and distribute it among the people. Poor families, too, sometimes do the same to fulfil a vow, often replacing the lamb with chicken to save money. Women work in teams to prepare this dish, because it needs to be stirred for hours until it has the consistency of melted cheese.*

PREPARATION: 15 MINS

COOKING: 3 HRS

SERVES 6

4 or 5 lamb shanks, fat removed

400g hulled wheat

3 onions

2 tablespoons vegetable oil

2 bay leaves

1 cinnamon stick

1 teaspoon mild pepper

Salt

1. Heat the oil in a casserole and sear the lamb shanks all over. Peel the onions, cut into quarters and add to the casserole with the cinnamon stick, bay leaves and 3 litres water. Bring to the boil; skim the froth from the surface. Cover and simmer gently for 2 hrs.
2. Take the lamb shanks out of the casserole, remove bones and skin. With a large spoon, skim off the fat rising to the surface of the stock. Replace the lamb in the stock and add the wheat. Cook for another hour on a low heat until the wheat is completely soft.
3. Stir regularly with a wooden spoon.
4. After cooking, season with salt and pepper and serve.

VARIATION

- *Chicken hrisseh.* Replace the lamb with a free-range chicken; the cooking time will be about 1 hour. Proceed with the recipe in the same way.

GOOD TO KNOW

- Hulled wheat is wheat without the husks. It is essential for this recipe as it is softer than the wheat sold in supermarkets. You can find it Middle-Eastern food shops or health food shops.
- This dish can be prepared the day before.
- For some families, cumin is indispensable to this recipe; it is added at the end, with the salt and pepper.

DAOUD BASHA

MINCED LAMB BALLS

This dish is named after a nobleman who must have been particularly fond of it. He was probably a pasha of Armenian extraction, the governor of Mount Lebanon in the 19th century.

PREPARATION: 20 MINS

COOKING: 30 MINS

SERVES 6

600g minced lamb
1 kg onions
100ml white wine vinegar
Vegetable oil
Salt and black pepper

1. Blend the meat with ½ teaspoon salt and ½ teaspoon pepper until it is reduced to a purée.
2. Shape the mixture into small balls 2.5cm in diameter and sauté for 5 minutes in a frying pan with a little oil.
3. Peel the onions and cut into wafer-thin slices.
4. In a large casserole, heat 2 teaspoons oil and sweat the onions for 10 minutes on a low flame.
5. Add the meatballs, vinegar and 100ml water.
6. Simmer, covered, for 20 minutes.
7. Serve with Basmati Rice or Rice with Vermicelli (see p. 77).

VARIATIONS

- In North Lebanon, a tomato-based sauce is used instead of the vinegar.
- You can also add 50g crushed walnuts to the meat and replace the vinegar with *debs remmane* (see p. 166).

BULGUR WHEAT WITH TOMATO

PREPARATION: 20 MINS

COOKING: 35 MINS

SERVES 6

400g coarse bulgur wheat (see p. 160)
300g minced lamb
50g pine nuts (see p. 163)
1 bunch flat-leaf parsley
500g onions
800ml tomato juice
1 level tablespoon 7 Spice Mix (see p. 165)
4 tablespoons vegetable oil
Salt

1. Finely shred the parsley, peel and chop the onions. Reserve separately.
2. Pour 4 tablespoons oil into a large casserole and sweat the onions. After a few minutes add the bulgur wheat and stir.
3. Add the tomato juice, 800ml water, salt and 7 Spice Mix.
4. Bring to the boil, cover, and simmer for 25 minutes, stirring from time to time.
5. In the meantime, dry-roast the pine nuts, add the meat and season with salt. Simmer for 10 minutes.
6. Serve the bulgur wheat with the meat and the pine nuts on top, sprinkled with chopped parsley.

VARIATIONS

- The minced meat can be replaced with a confit of 2 lamb shanks or simply with roasted lamb shanks.
- This recipe can be made without meat, as a side dish.
- You can also use fresh, peeled tomatoes.

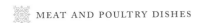

MASBAHT-EL-DARWISH

The name of this dish means 'the dervish's rosary', no doubt because the vegetables resemble colourful beads.

PREPARATION: 20 MINS

SWEATING: 1 NIGHT

COOKING: 30–35 MINS

SERVES 6

3 courgettes

3 aubergines

3 potatoes

3 tomatoes

3 carrots

2 onions

2 garlic cloves

1 red pepper

200g green beans

400g shoulder of lamb, deboned

2 tablespoons *debs remmane* (pomegranate molasses, see p. 166)

Vegetable oil

Salt and black pepper

THE DAY BEFORE

1. Peel the aubergines and cut in half widthways, then each half into four. Sprinkle with salt and leave to sweat in a colander in the fridge.

ON THE DAY

2. Cut the courgettes in two lengthways, then each half into four pieces. Peel the potatoes and cut into two or three pieces each. Peel and chop the carrots.
3. In a saucepan or a frying pan, fry the courgettes, aubergines, potatoes and carrots for 3 minutes. Set aside on kitchen paper.
4. Peel the onions and the garlic. Chop the onions and crush the garlic.
5. Cut the pepper into juliennes (thin batons).
6. Top and tail the green beans.
7. Peel the tomatoes, de-seed and cut into eight pieces.
8. Preheat the oven to 180ºC (gas mark 6).
9. Chop the meat into 3cm cubes. Pour a little oil into a frying pan and sear the meat on all sides. Reserve.
10. Sauté the onions, garlic and pepper in a little oil. Add the tomatoes, salt and pepper.
11. Place the meat and all the vegetables in an ovenproof dish.
12. Add water to half fill the dish, drizzle *debs remmane* evenly over the whole dish.
13. Cook in the oven for 20 minutes.
14. Serve piping hot.

GOOD TO KNOW

- You can prepare this dish in advance and place it in the oven 20 minutes before sitting down to eat.

Fish Dishes

SAYADIEH

This is a fisherman's dish; sayad samak – literally "fish hunter" – is what we call a fisherman. Originally sayadieh would be made with left-over scraps of fish combined with rice, to which onions and various seasonings would be added. These days, it is a dish for special occasions made with sea bass or other firm-fleshed fish. Traditionally there are two kinds of sayadieh, white and brown. The only difference is the way the onion is cooked: just to golden in the former, and almost burnt in the latter, which gives the rice a deep brown colour.

PREPARATION: 15 MINS

COOKING: 55 MINS

SERVES 6

1 sea bass about 2kg, scaled and gutted or in fillets
300g basmati rice
8 onions
1 tablespoon caraway seeds
2 tablespoons ground cumin
50g pine nuts (see p. 163)
150ml olive oil
1 litre fish stock
100ml vegetable oil
Salt

FOR THE SAUCE:

1 tablespoon flour
A knob of butter
Juice of ½ lemon

VARIATIONS

You can use cod or monkfish instead of sea bass. You may also like to add saffron to the onions' cooking liquid.

This dish can also be served with a Tajine Sauce (see p. 29).

GARNISH

1. Dry-roast the pine nuts until golden and put aside.
2. Peel 2 onions, halve and slice finely into half-moons.
3. Pour the vegetable oil into a frying-pan over medium heat. When hot, add the sliced onions. Stir constantly until they are crispy and golden.
4. Remove them from the pan and spread them out on kitchen paper to draw off excess oil. Leave them open to the air and put to one side.
5. Peel and roughly chop the 6 remaining onions. Pour the olive oil into a saucepan and fry the onions over a high flame until they begin to brown.
6. Add to this the fish stock, spices and salt. Lower the heat and simmer for 20 minutes. Then drain the onions and reserve the liquid.
7. Pre-heat the oven to 200°C (gas mark 6–7).

RICE

8. Heat a little oil in a saucepan. Briefly fry the rice in this, then add 500ml of the cooking liquid from the onions. Bring to the boil, cover and cook for 15 minutes on a low flame. Then remove from the heat and leave covered.

FISH

9. While the rice is cooking, salt your fish (if whole) and bake in the oven for 30 minutes.
10. If you are using fillets instead, fry them over a medium heat in a non-stick pan, skin down, without oil or other fat.

SAUCE

11. While the fish and rice are cooking, melt the knob of butter in a pan and brown the flour. Add the rest of the onions' cooking liquid, heat until it bubbles gently and add the lemon juice before serving.
12. Present the rice with the pieces of fish, onions and roasted pine-nuts stacked together, and the sauce on the side.

ROYAL SEA BREAM WITH AUBERGINE

PREPARATION: 15 MINS

SWEATING: 1 NIGHT

COOKING: 10 MINS

SERVES 6

900g fillets of "royal" or gilthead bream
3 aubergines
2 tablespoons of *debs remmane* (see p. 166)
Plain white flour
400g basmati rice
Vegetable oil
Salt and pepper

THE DAY BEFORE

1. Halve the aubergines lengthways, then cut each half into four pieces. Salt generously and leave in a colander in a cool place overnight.

ON THE DAY

2. Cut the royal bream fillets into two, length-ways. Season with salt and pepper and lightly sprinkle with flour.
3. Heat the oil in a frying-pan. First fry the aubergines for 7 minutes, then remove them and fry the fish for 3 minutes. Set aubergines and fish on kitchen paper to absorb some of the oil.
4. Arrange the fillets of bream and the aubergines in a dish. Trickle *debs remmane* over both fish and aubergines. Serve with Basmati Rice (see p. 77)

COMMENT

Two vegetable dishes go very well with this sea bream:

- Aubergines: mix together 300g of Moutabal (see p. 27) and the seeds of 1 pomegranate, 2 tablespoons *debs remmane* and a bunch of chives, chopped.
- Tomatoes: combine 6 tomatoes, peeled, de-seeded and diced, with 1 finely chopped shallot and 2 tablespoons *debs remmane*.

SPICY GREY MULLET

PREPARATION: 15 MINS

COOKING: 15 MINS

SERVES 6

1.5kg grey mullet fillets
3 bunches coriander
1 whole bulb of garlic
2 onions
Juice of 2 lemons
1 tablespoon powdered cumin
A pinch of powdered chilli, or more to taste
Vegetable oil
Salt

1. Remove the skin from the fillets and cut them into 2cm-long pieces.
2. Peel the onions. Coarsely chop them and the coriander.
3. Separate the garlic cloves and peel. Chop each clove into 4 or 5 pieces.
4. Brown the onions in a little oil in a high-sided frying-pan. Add the garlic and cook for 3 minutes, then add the coriander.
5. Add the fish, the salt and cumin.
6. Pour in water to come half-way up the fish and vegetables, cover and simmer over a low heat for 5 minutes.
7. Add the chilli and lemon juice and serve warm as a *mezze* dish.

OCTOPUS SALAD WITH CORIANDER

PREPARATION: 15 MINS

COOKING: 45 MINS

SERVES 6

2kg medium-sized octopus, cleaned

2 onions

3 cloves of garlic

2 bunches coriander

3 tomatoes

Olive oil

Salt and black pepper

1. Chop the octopus into 3cm sections.
2. Peel the onions and garlic. Chop the onions and crush the garlic.
3. Separate the coriander leaves from the stalks; set the leaves aside and tie the stalks together into a bundle.
4. Brown the onions and garlic in the olive oil in a saucepan; add the octopus, salt and pepper to taste and the bundle of coriander stalks. Simmer, covered, for 45 minutes on a low heat.
5. Take out the coriander stalks and leave the rest to cool.
6. Dice the tomatoes (unpeeled) and finely chop the coriander leaves.
7. Mix the octopus, coriander and tomatoes together. Serve.

SQUID WITH GARLIC AND CORIANDER

PREPARATION: 10 MINS

COOKING: 20 MINS

SERVES 6

2kg medium-sized squid
2 bunches coriander
3 cloves of garlic
1 tablespoon olive oil
Salt and black pepper

1. Clean the squid. Chop the main body and wings into rings; separate the tentacles from the rest but keep them whole.
2. Peel and crush the garlic.
3. Finely chop the coriander.
4. Put the olive oil, squid and garlic in a saucepan, and add pepper and salt to taste. Cover and cook over a low heat for 20 minutes.
5. Remove from heat and mix in the coriander. Serve with Basmati Rice (see p. 77) or with boiled ratte or other waxy potatoes.

SABBIDIJ

CUTTLEFISH IN INK

PREPARATION: 5 MINS

COOKING: 55 MINS

SERVES 6

2kg medium-sized cuttlefish,
cleaned
1 clove of garlic
1 ink sachet
Salt and black pepper

1. Peel and crush the garlic.
2. Put the cuttlefish and garlic in a saucepan. Pour in 100ml water and leave to simmer, covered, on a low heat, for 45 minutes.
3. Add the ink, salt and pepper, and leave to cook, uncovered, for a further 10 minutes.
4. Serve at room temperature or cold.

VARIATION

• You could add a little orange or mandarin zest to the squid-ink.

COMMENT

• If your cuttlefish are large, cut them into 5cm-long sections.

GOOD TO KNOW

• All good fishmongers will supply sachets of cuttlefish ink, although you may need to order in advance.

THE SULTAN OF FISH

WITH DEEP-FRIED CAULIFLOWER AND AUBERGINE

In Lebanon many different fish may be deep-fried. Allow 300g fish per person, 200g if you are using anchovies, sardines or other small fish, or 150g for squid. The best for deep-frying is red mullet, which indeed can be called "Sultan Ibrahim", because, it is said, this fish used to be the Ottoman ruler's favourite food.

PREPARATION: 5 MINS

SWEATING: 2–3 HRS (OR OVERNIGHT)

COOKING: 5 MINS

SERVES 6

1.5kg of a selection of fish, all gutted and de-scaled
2 aubergines
1 small cauliflower
3 pitta bread (see p. 161)
Plain white flour
Frying oil
Salt and pepper

1. Peel the aubergines and slice lengthways into 4mm-thick ovals. Put them in a colander, salt and leave for 2 to 3 hours in a cool place to draw out the bitter juices. This step can be done the day before and the aubergines set aside overnight.
2. Season with salt, pepper and lightly flour the fish.
3. Heat the oil in a high-sided pan. Once it is very hot, immerse the fish for 2 minutes.
4. Take out the fish and pat with kitchen paper to remove excess oil.
5. Cut the pitta bread into 2cm-thick slices and fry until golden.
6. Rinse off and dry the aubergines, then fry until they are soft and melting.
7. Divide the cauliflower into small florets and fry until they turn a fine golden colour.
8. Serve the fish hot, with the fried bread squares and vegetables.

COMMENT

- Tarator Sauce (see p. 29) goes well with this dish, as does *debs remmane* (see p. 166). Or you can simply squeeze a lemon and drizzle its juice and a little olive oil over everything.

FISH FREEKEH

PREPARATION: 15 MINS

COOKING: 55 MINS

SERVES 6

300g *freekeh* (see p. 168)
200g red mullet fillets
500g sea bass fillets
6 king prawns
2 onions
2 cloves of garlic
1 carrot
900ml fish stock
Vegetable oil
Salt and black pepper

1. Peel the carrot, onions and garlic. Chop the onions, dice the carrot and crush the garlic.
2. Heat a little vegetable oil in a high-sided frying-pan and brown the onion and garlic. Add the *freekeh*, stock, and salt and pepper; cover and leave to simmer gently for 45 minutes.
3. In the mean time, cut each fish fillet into three pieces.
4. When the *freekeh* is nearly ready, heat some vegetable oil in a separate pan. When hot, add the fish fillets and the unpeeled prawns. Sear them rapidly on all sides, then add the fish and prawns to the *freekeh* along with the diced carrot.
5. Allow to cook for a further 5 minutes. Serve, perhaps garnished with a sprig of dill.

Sweets

It is traditional to eat fruit at the end of a Lebanese meal. Sweets and sweet dishes
are savoured at other times of day, often in the afternoon, and occasionally in
the morning. Most Lebanese cities have a number of vast patisseries, which are
considered secular family institutions and cultivate their fine reputations. Generally,
we distinguish between sweets made at home and those – often much more
difficult to make – which can only be bought in the patisseries. We have limited
our selection here to sweet dishes that can successfully be made at home, and also
those we have found most suitable for serving as dessert or alongside tea or coffee.

HAYTALIYEH

This traditional Ottoman dish is flavoured with orange-blossom water and mastic, which is the resin from the lentisk or mastic tree found principally on the Greek island of Chios. The transparent resin weeps down the length of the trees, turning white only on prolonged contact with the air and hardening on the trunks, from where it is collected. This precious sap was once reserved for the imperial harem at Constantinople, but the custom of "masticking" became widespread in several cities in Western Europe, where wealthy women paid fortunes for it, convinced that it would make their teeth whiter. In Lebanon and many other Eastern Mediterranean countries, mastic still features in numerous sweet dishes – patisserie, ice creams, drinks and confectionery.

PREPARATION: 10 MINS

COOKING: 10 MINS

SERVES 6

FOR THE HAYTALIYEH

1 litre full-fat milk

75g corn flour

5g mastic

100ml orange-blossom water (see p. 169)

A pinch of sugar

FOR THE SYRUP

100ml orange juice

Zest of 1 orange

200g caster sugar

1. Crush the mastic with the pinch of sugar – this makes it easier to crush to powder. Pour the milk into a heavy-bottomed saucepan, heat and whisk as it comes to boiling. Make a paste by adding a little water to the corn flour and add this to the milk; continue whisking.
2. Bring to the boil again and remove from the heat. Now stir in the orange-blossom water and the mastic – if these are added over heat the mixture will become bitter.
3. Pour into ramekins.
4. Using a peeler, strip the zest from the orange and chop finely, keeping a few long sections aside.
5. Take a saucepan for the syrup. Pour in the orange juice, the sugar and the zest and heat on a high flame for 10 minutes. Leave this to cool.
6. To serve, sprinkle each filled ramekin with the zest strips reserved earlier, then pour a little syrup over each.

VARIATIONS

- You can make the syrup with other fruit, such as strawberries.
- If you add sugar and an extra 25g of corn flour to the milk, you will make *mouhallabieh*. This dish is served without syrup because it is already sweetened. You can decorate it with sprinklings of ground pistachios.

GOOD TO KNOW

- If you are unable to find mastic (it is sold in small packets rather as saffron is) in Middle-Eastern food shops, you can simply leave it out of the recipe.

WALNUT MARZIPAN CAKE

COOKING: 25 MINS

SERVES 6

360g ground almonds
300g icing sugar
75ml orange-blossom water
(see p. 169)

FOR THE FILLING

250g walnuts
100g icing sugar
35ml rose water (see p. 169)

1. Pre-heat the oven to 120°C (gas-mark 4)
2. To prepare the filling, roughly blend the walnuts in a food processor with the icing sugar and rose water, then set aside.
3. Blend the ground almonds, icing sugar and orange-blossom water. You should obtain a ball of pastry that comes away from the sides of the food processor. Divide this into two.
4. Lay out the two pieces of pastry in the middle of large squares of greaseproof paper. Roll them out into squares about 2mm thick. Spread the walnut filling over one of the squares of pastry. Cover the filling with the other piece of pastry. Decorate the top surface by drawing designs onto it with a fork or knife.
5. Place on a baking tray and bake in the oven for 25 minutes.
6. Once removed from the oven, leave the cake to cool. Then cut into 2cm squares to serve.

VARIATION

- You can substitute pistachios for the walnuts.

COMMENT

- This recipe can be made into individual bite-size cakes (see photo p. 152). To do this, divide the pastry into four sections instead of two and roll each section into a thick sausage. Flatten the pastry "sausages" into rectangles. Spread the filling in the middle of each, roll them into cylinders and cut into slices of about 2cm width. Bake in your pre-heated oven for 15 minutes.

MEGHLI

Meghli is traditionally made to celebrate the birth of a baby. It is offered to friends and family who come to congratulate the new parents. In the Bekaa valley in eastern Lebanon, it is known as caraway, *"caraway", when cold, and* meghli, *"boiled", when it is served hot. It used to be said that the spices in this sweet dish would stimulate the mother's milk.*

PREPARATION: 5 MINS

COOKING: 15 MINS

SERVES 6

150g rice semolina
3 tablespoons ground caraway seeds
3 tablespoons ground cinnamon
200g caster sugar
50g grated coconut
50g pine nuts (see p. 163)
50 g unsalted, shelled pistachios
50g blanched almonds

1. Soak the pine nuts, pistachios and almonds in tepid water.
2. In a flame-proof casserole dish, combine the rice semolina, the caraway, cinnamon and sugar. Then cover with a litre of water and bring to the boil, stirring regularly. Cover the casserole and leave to cook over a low heat for 12 minutes.
3. Pour this mixture into ramekins. Leave these to cool, then place in the fridge.
4. Remove the nuts from the water and dry off thoroughly.
5. Present the ramekins with a topping of sprinkled, grated coconut, almonds, pistachios and whole pine nuts.

VARIATION

- ½ teaspoon of aniseed can be added to the spice mixture, if you like the taste.

GOOD TO KNOW

- You will find rice semolina in good Middle-Eastern food shops.

ATAYEF-BIL-ASHTA

Several kinds of Lebanese pastries are filled with a thick, milky white cream called ashta. *This cream is made with milk set to boil in a large pan. A delicate skin forms on the milk's surface, which is then skimmed off with a ladle and kept in a bowl in the fridge. This process is repeated over several hours, until there is no liquid milk left in the pan. There is now a range of alternatives to this process, such as using crème fraiche mixed with fresh white breadcrumbs or semolina cooked in the milk as substitutes for ashta. We feel the recipe below comes closest to recreating its traditional taste.*

PREPARATION: 20 MINS

**FOR THE PASTRY TO RISE:
1HR**

COOKING: 15–20 MINS

SERVES 6

FOR THE PASTRY
180g fine white flour
400ml water
12g baking powder

FOR THE CREAM
100g mozzarella
300g mascarpone
2 tablespoons orange-
blossom water (see p. 169)
20g caster sugar

FOR THE SYRUP
100ml water
200g caster sugar
1 tablespoon orange-blossom
water

TO DECORATE
20g chopped pistachios

1. Combine the flour, water and baking powder. Leave in a warm place to rise for 1 hour.
2. Meanwhile, pulse one cheese then the other briefly in a food processor. Whisk them together with the sugar and orange-blossom water then put aside in a cool place.
3. For the syrup, put the water and sugar in a saucepan and cook for 10 minutes on a medium heat. Then remove from the heat and add the orange-blossom water; leave to cool.
4. When the hour is up, heat a crêpe pan or other small, non-stick frying pan. Cook a ladle-full of the pastry mixture on one side only for about 2 mins, to make a small, thick crêpe pancake, and repeat until the mixture is used up.
5. Shape the crêpes into cones by pinching two edges together with the uncooked face on the inside. Fill each cone generously with the cheese mixture. Scatter the pistachios over each cone and then drizzle with orange-blossom syrup.

VARIATIONS
- You can make the pastry mixture using baker's yeast instead of baking powder.
- You can replace the classic orange-blossom syrup with another fruit-flavoured syrup.

EASTER MAAMOUL

This is an Eastertide sweet in Lebanon, prepared by Christian families during holy week and offered to family and friends visiting for the holiday. The dough is prepared a day early, as are the different fillings. The next day, everyone – usually women – gathers around a large platter to make the maamoul, *which requires special tools used only for this recipe and then laid aside until the following year. These consist of wooden moulds, usually 4–6cm in diameter, whose different shapes indicate the different fillings of each* maamoul. *If it is rounded and conical, it is for a walnut* maamoul; *if rounded but flat, the filling is dates; if more ovoid it will be pistachio… These conventions are always adhered to, as is the ritual of preparation, although recipes may differ from one family to the next. This is the recipe used by Andrée's mother and sisters.*

PREPARATION: 3 HRS

PASTRY RESTING TIME: 1 NIGHT + 2 HRS

COOKING: 10 MINS PER BATCH

FOR 60 SMALL MAAMOUL

250g fine semolina

250g medium semolina

200g butter

2 tablespoons *mahlab* (see p. 144)

50ml orange-blossom water (see p. 169)

50ml rose water (see p. 169)

FOR THE FILLINGS

125g walnuts, coarsely chopped

125g unsalted, shelled whole pistachios

125g dates

A knob of butter

4 tablespoons caster sugar

2 tablespoons orange-blossom water

THE DAY BEFORE

1. Melt the butter in a small pan. In a large bowl, knead together the two kinds of semolina, the *mahlab* and the melted butter. Cover and set aside at room temperature.

ON THE DAY

2. Pre-heat the oven to 220°C (gas mark 7–8).
3. Gently warm the orange-blossom water and rose water. Make a hollow in the semolina and pour in the two flavoured waters; mix in until the semolina has become a smooth pastry dough. Leave aside for 2 hours.
4. Prepare each filling separately:
5. Mix the crushed walnuts with 2 tablespoons of sugar and 1 tablespoon of orange-blossom water.
6. Mix the crushed pistachios with 2 tablespoons of sugar and 1 tablespoon of orange-blossom water.
7. Blend the dates into a purée, either process or rub in the butter thoroughly and then roll this mixture into balls of about 2cm diameter, or 4cm, if you are using large moulds.
8. Now take a piece from the big lump of semolina pastry, shape into a small ball and then both flatten and hollow it so that it can be wrapped right around a spoonful of one of the three fillings.
9. Press the filled ball into the appropriate mould, then tap it out cleanly onto the table. Lay it straight away on an ovenproof sheet.
10. Bake for 10 minutes in the middle of the oven, using the fan-assisted function if possible.

GOOD TO KNOW

- It is possible to make these special biscuits without a mould: shape into filled balls, then pinch with tweezers to give the characteristic ridged appearance (see photograph).
- The *mahlab* plant is also known as "prunus mahaleb", or perfumed cherry; also as St Lucie cherry.

AWAMATS

DOUGHNUTS IN SYRUP

PREPARATION: 5 MINS

RESTING TIME: 30 MINS

COOKING: 15 MINS

SERVES 6

FOR THE DOUGH

300g ewe's-milk yoghurt
150g fine white flour
A pinch bicarbonate of soda
Light vegetable oil for frying

FOR THE SYRUP

100ml water
200g caster sugar
1 tablespoon orange-blossom
water (see p. 169)

1. To make the dough, combine the yoghurt, flour and bicarbonate of soda. Leave for 30 minutes at room temperature.
2. For the syrup, pour the water and sugar into a saucepan and heat together for 10 minutes. Then remove from the heat and add the orange-blossom water.
3. When dough and syrup are ready, shape the dough into balls. Bring the oil in your deep-fryer to 160°C and fry the doughnuts for 5 minutes. Remove them from the fryer and allow any excess oil to drain off, then immerse in syrup.

VARIATIONS

- *Awamats* can be made with flour, baker's yeast and water, instead of bicarbonate of soda. The dough should have the consistency of thick cream.
- You may also replace 50g of the flour with potato flour.

KHSHEIF

Rose-scented salad of dried apricots and nuts

PREPARATION: 10 MINS

SOAKING TIME: 1 NIGHT

ASSEMBLING THE DISH:

10 MINS

COOLING TIME: 4 HRS

SERVES 6

200g dried apricots
200g prunes
50g sultanas
100g currants
50g pine nuts (see p. 163)
50g unsalted shelled
pistachios
50g whole blanched almonds
50ml orange-blossom water
(see p. 169)
50ml rose water (see p. 169)

THE DAY BEFORE

1. In separate bowls, leave the currants, pistachios, almonds and pine nuts to soak in a litre of cold water, covered, for a full night, so that they soften.

ON THE DAY

2. Without draining away the water, add the apricots, prunes and sultanas, the rose and orange-blossom waters to the bowl of currants, then leave aside in a cool place.
3. Drain the almonds, the pistachios and the pine nuts.
4. Remove the pistachios' skins.
5. Add the pine nuts, almonds and pistachios to the dried fruit mixture and set aside to cool for 4 hours – until it is time to serve the dish.

VARIATIONS

* This dish was originally made just with dried apricots; prunes have been added more recently.
* Other dried fruits can be added, such as figs, pears, cherries, even peaches.
* You can also leave out the pine nuts, almonds and pistachios, according to your taste.

SNAYNIYEH

This wheat-based dessert is traditionally made to celebrate a child cutting its first tooth.

PREPARATION: 20 MINS

SOAKING TIME: 1 NIGHT

COOKING: 30 MINS

SERVES 6

200g hulled wheat

2 pomegranates

50g pine nuts (see p. 163)

50g whole almonds

50g unsalted, shelled
pistachios

100g caster sugar

100ml orange-blossom water
(p. 169)

THE DAY BEFORE

1. In separate bowls, leave the pistachios, almonds and pine nuts to soak in cold water.

ON THE DAY

2. Cook the wheat for 30 minutes, covered, in boiling water.
3. When 30 minutes is nearly up, add the sugar and orange-blossom water. Stir thoroughly.
4. Scoop the seeds out of the pomegranates. Remove the skins of the almonds and pistachios.
5. Mix all the ingredients together and serve in glasses or a glass bowl.

GOOD TO KNOW

• Hulled wheat is wheat that has had the outer husk removed. It is essential in this recipe to achieve a smooth, melting texture; ordinary supermarket wheat will not do. You will find hulled wheat in Middle-Eastern food shops and health-food shops. If pomegranates are not in season, the recipe can be made without them.

STRAWBERRY AND ORANGE-BLOSSOM SALAD

PREPARATION: 15 MINS

COOLING: 2 HRS

COOKING: 10 MINS

SERVES 6

500g strawberries

1 lemon (unwaxed)

1 tablespoon red wine vinegar

100g caster sugar

100ml orange juice

40ml orange-blossom water (see p. 169)

1. Wash the strawberries and hull them. Chop them into a bowl, dividing each into three or four pieces, then add the vinegar and half the sugar. Mix and leave in a cool place for 1 hour.
2. Peel zest from the lemon, using a peeler or zester, and chop. Put the zest into a saucepan and cover with water. Add the remaining sugar. Squeeze some juice from the lemon and add 1 tablespoon to the saucepan.
3. Simmer on a low flame for 10 minutes, then set aside.
4. Pour the orange juice and orange-blossom water into a jug and mix. Pour the mixed juice over the strawberries and leave them in a cool place to absorb the flavours for a further hour.
5. Serve sprinkled with the candied lemon zest.

KARIM'S TWIST

Add a pinch of salt to the water while cooking the zest.

PEARS IN ARAK

PREPARATION: 10 MINS

COOKING: 25 MINS

SERVES 6

6 firm Comice pears
200g caster sugar
Juice of ½ lemon
100ml *arak*
1 tablespoon carob molasses
(see p. 166)

1. Peel the pears and remove the pips – preferably by removing the core from beneath using a peeler or corer, thus leaving the fruit whole. Submerge in water in a large saucepan. Add the lemon juice, half the sugar and half the *arak*. Cook for 20 minutes on a low heat, then set aside.
2. Remove 50 ml of the cooking liquid and instead pour in the remaining sugar and *arak*. Cook for a further 5 minutes.
3. Serve the pears topped with the syrup obtained in the cooking process, and with carob molasses drizzled on top.

GOOD TO KNOW

- Lebanese *arak* is a grape alcohol to which star anise has been added during distillation for flavour. It is not to be confused with Sri Lankan *arak*, which is a spirit made from coconuts, or with *arak* from Réunion Island, which is their name for rum.
- You will find carob molasses in good Middle-Eastern food shops.

MAAKAROUN

It is no coincidence that this sweet biscuit's name sounds so similar to our macaroon, for they share a common ancestor: the Italian maccarone, a term which originally referred to small pastries similar to gnocchi. Indeed, the Lebanese maakaroun *is reminiscent of gnocchi – in outward appearance only, of course, for the taste is quite different. These days available all year round, as a feast-day sweet* maakarouns *used to be made for Eid el-Barbarah, Saint Barbara's feast, on the 4th December.*

PREPARATION: 20 MINS

COOLING: 30 MINS

COOKING: 40 MINS

SERVES 6

FOR THE PASTRY

250g fine white flour
1 teaspoon *mahlab*
1 teaspoon ground aniseed
1 teaspoon raising agent
100ml vegetable oil
100ml water

FOR THE SYRUP

450g icing sugar
250ml water
1 tablespoon orange-blossom
water (see p. 169)
Approx 500ml frying oil

PASTRY

1. Combine the flour, vegetable oil, *mahlab* aniseed, raising agent and water, mixing until you achieve a smooth pastry. Leave in a cool place for 30 minutes.
2. Divide the pastry into quarters. Shape each quarter into a thick cigar-roll of about 2cm diameter, then cut into 4cm-long sections.
3. Take a wicker basket or table mat and roll the small dough cigars along the inner surface, pushing them against the sides. (This is the same way gnocchi are made.) This action hollows out the centre of the dough and therefore to helps it to cook evenly throughout.

SYRUP

4. Boil the water and sugar together until you have a medium syrup, neither too thick nor too runny. Remove from the heat and add the orange-blossom water.
5. Now heat the frying oil in a high-sided pan. When it is very hot, add 8 – 10 *maakarouns* at a time, depending on the size of your pan, and fry until they are a light golden colour. Turn over to fry the other side. Now quickly remove them from the pan and straight away immerse them in the syrup, warm or cold as you prefer. After 3 minutes, remove from the syrup and place in a dish to serve. Repeat this process until all the *maakarouns* are fried.

VARIATION

• Imported sugar used not to be widely available in Lebanon, especially in the villages; grape or carob molasses was used instead (see pp. 166 and 167). The latter being of a thicker consistency than syrup, it requires the addition of a little water so that the *maakarouns* can absorb it.

COMMENTS

• *Mahlab* is also known as "prunus mahaleb" or perfumed cherry, or even sometimes 'St Lucie's cherry'. It is the kernel of this cherry that we use for cooking. You can buy it in Middle-Eastern food shops, whole or in ground form. To keep it as fresh as possible, it is advisable to buy it whole and then grind as needed.

APPLES AND BANANAS WITH CINNAMON

In Lebanon, the banana and apple plantations are only 30 km apart, the former being found along the coastline, the latter on higher ground inland. This proximity is a rare opportunity; it inspired us to combine the two flavours.

PREPARATION: 10 MINS

COOKING: 15 MINS

SERVES 6

9 apples, different varieties
2 bananas
1 tablespoon ground
cinnamon

TO ACCOMPANY:

6 scoops of cinnamon ice
cream

1. Peel the apples, core and slice them.
2. Peel and slice the bananas.
3. Put all the fruit in a saucepan with a small cupful of water. Cover and cook on a low heat for 15 minutes.
4. Halfway through cooking, add the cinnamon.
5. Serve hot with a scoop of cinnamon ice cream per person.

RIZ-BI-HALIB

LEBANESE RICE PUDDING

PREPARATION: 10 MINS

COOKING: 25 MINS

COOLING: 2 HRS

SERVES 6

100g pudding rice
200ml water
1 litre whole milk
70g caster sugar
30g cornflour
50ml orange-blossom water
(see p. 169)

1. Pour the rice into a saucepan and cover with the water; bring to boiling. Turn down the heat and cook uncovered for 20 min.
2. When the rice is cooked, pour the milk into a separate, large saucepan and bring to the boil. Add the rice and the remaining cooking liquid as well as the cornflour. Once again heat to boiling.
3. Remove from the heat and add the sugar and orange-blossom water. Stir well.
4. Pour the mixture into ramekins and leave to set for 2 hours in the refrigerator. Serve chilled.

COMMENT

*   Rice puddings can be served with a fruit syrup or plain sugar syrup.

OSMALLIEH

For this sweet confection of osmanli (Ottoman) origin, a special pastry rather like vermicelli or angel hair pasta is required. It can be found in Middle-Eastern food shops, by the name of cheayriyeh, *usually in semi-dried form.*

PREPARATION: 30 MINS

COOLING: 1 NIGHT

COOKING: 50 MINS

SERVES 8

FOR THE PASTRY

300g *cheayriyeh*

75g butter

100ml vegetable oil

FOR THE FILLING

150g mozzarella

400g mascarpone

50ml orange-blossom water

(see p. 169)

10g caster sugar

FOR THE SYRUP

350g caster sugar

150ml water

50g unsalted, shelled

pistachios

1 tablespoon orange-blossom

water

1 tablespoon rose water

Juice of 1 lemon

KARIM'S TWIST

When cherries are in season, de-stone 300g and stew them while you are making the syrup. Take half the cherries and add to the osmallieh's filling. Mix the rest with the syrup (see photograph on facing page).

THE DAY BEFORE

PASTRY

1. Melt the butter and mix with the oil.
2. Unwrap the *cheayriyeh* pastry. Take out 300g of it and put all remaining pastry in the freezer to keep. Carefully mix the butter-and-oil liquid into the pastry you are using, so that all strands are evenly coated and the pastry can be spread out quite smoothly.
3. Take two tart tins each of 30cm diameter and line with grease-proof paper so that the paper laps generously over the sides of the tins.
4. Divide the pastry in half and spread out in the two tart tins. Pat it down evenly and compactly so that it covers the base of each tin. Set aside in a cool place.

SYRUP

5. Boil the sugar and water together in a saucepan. Add 1 tablespoon of lemon juice to prevent the sugar crystallising. The syrup must only thicken slightly, so remove the pan from the heat while it is still quite runny.
6. Next add the orange-blossom and rose waters. Mix and leave the syrup to cool, then cover.

FILLING

7. Give each cheese a few seconds in the food processor. Then whisk them together along with the sugar and orange-blossom water. Cover and set in a cool place.

ON THE DAY

8. Pre-heat the oven to 150°C (gas mark 6). Bake each of the pastry "tarts" in turn for 30 minutes, until they are golden.
9. While the second tart is baking, use the first one's greaseproof paper edges to help you lift it out of its dish. Slide it onto a large round platter of at least 50cm diameter.
10. Using a tablespoon, gently spread the filling out over the now crunchy *cheayriyeh* pastry, taking care not to crush it. Cover the whole circle of pastry with filling.
11. When the second tart is ready, again use the greaseproof paper edges to help you lift it out of its tin and slide it gently on top of the layer of filling.
12. Grind the pistachios finely and sprinkle over the whole surface of the *osmallieh*.
13. Serve with the syrup in a separate jug.

Ice Cream

Frozen sweets have for centuries had a favoured place in Levantine cookery, as demonstrated by words like sorbet, which comes from the Arabic root for "drink" – the same root that gives us "syrup" and "sherbet". One of the iconic Lebanese ice creams requires an ingredient known as *sahlab* or *salep*, which is the ivory-coloured powder of a particular orchid bulb and has powerful emulsifying properties. Traditionally the ice cream would be whipped until it became unctuous and sticky, then served in rectangular "cones", filled to overflowing and dusted with ground pistachio nuts. The recipes that follow here also include a halva ice cream invented by Karim, a strawberry and a rose ice cream; this last flavour can also be made into a sorbet. If you are able to get hold of *sahlab* while visiting the Middle East, it is better to buy it in small quantities – 200g for instance – because only a little is needed in each recipe (1 tablespoon for 1 litre of milk) and also because it quickly goes off. To keep it fresh, store in an airtight container in the refrigerator. This ingredient can also be found in Middle-Eastern food shops, but there it is often sold already mixed with sugar and powdered milk. We have adjusted the recipes with this in mind.

HALVA ICE CREAM

PREPARATION: 30 MINS

SERVES 6

400g plain halva
900ml whole or half-fat milk
30ml double cream
100g fructose

1. Blend the halva, fructose and double cream in a food processor until they form a smooth cream.
2. Pour the milk into a heavy-based saucepan and add the halva mixture.
3. Bring to boiling, stirring constantly with a wooden spatula. Remove from the heat and leave to cool.
4. Once the mixture is cool, pour half into your ice-cream maker and set it going for 30 minutes, or until ice cream has formed. Keep the other half of the mixture cool while the first batch of ice cream is being made. When this batch is ready, scoop your ice cream into a serving bowl and replace with the other half of the mixture, to prepare in the same way.
5. Serve and eat immediately.

VARIATION

• Halva itself is sufficiently sweet that you may feel you do not need the fructose. If you prefer, you can leave it out or replace it with 10g of caster sugar.

STRAWBERRY ICE CREAM

PREPARATION: 30 MINS

SERVES 6

400g strawberries
300ml whole or half-fat milk
150ml double cream
80g caster sugar
70g *sahlab* (see p. 149)

1. Wash the strawberries, drain and hull. Mix them with the sugar, blend in a food processor and set the purée aside in a cool place.
2. Pour the milk into a heavy-based saucepan, then add the cream and the *sahlab*. Bring to boiling, stirring constantly with a wooden spatula. Once the mixture has boiled, remove from the heat and leave to cool.
3. Stir this cream mixture into the strawberry purée.
4. Once the mixture is cool, pour half into your ice-cream maker and set it going for 30 minutes, or until ice cream has formed. Keep the other half of the mixture cold while the first batch of ice cream is being made. When this batch is ready, scoop your ice cream into a serving bowl and replace with the other half of the mixture, to prepare in the same way.
5. Serve and eat immediately.

COMMENTS

• The *sahlab* available in shops tends to be already sweetened. If you are lucky enough to find pure *sahlab* powder, you will need to replace the 70g *sahlab* specified above with the following mixture: 1 tablespoon *sahlab* powder and 150g sugar.

SAHLAB ICE CREAM

PREPARATION: 30 MINS

SERVES 6

250g *sahlab* (see p. 149)
900ml whole or half-fat milk
150ml double cream
50ml orange-blossom water
(see p. 169)
1 teaspoon caster sugar
3–4 mastic tears (if you are
unable to find mastic in your
local Middle-Eastern shops,
you can leave it out of this
recipe)

1. Using a pestle and mortar, crush the mastic tears thoroughly into the sugar and set aside.
2. Mix together the *sahlab*, milk and cream.
3. Pour the mixture into a heavy-based saucepan and bring to the boil, stirring constantly with a wooden spatula.
4. Remove from the heat, add the ground sugar and mastic and the orange-blossom water, and leave to cool.
5. Once the mixture is cool, pour half into your ice-cream maker and set it going for 30 minutes, or until ice cream has formed. Keep the other half of the mixture cold while the first batch of ice cream is being made. When this batch is ready, scoop your ice cream into a serving bowl and replace with the other half of the mixture, to prepare in the same way.
6. Serve and eat immediately.

COMMENTS

- The *sahlab* that is sold in most shops tends to be ready-mixed with sugar and milk powder. If by chance you have pure *sahlab* powder, you will need to substitute the 70g *sahlab* specified above with the following mixture: 1 tablespoon *sahlab* powder and 150g sugar.

ROSE ICE CREAM

PREPARATION: 30 MINS

SERVES 6

900ml whole or half-fat milk
70g *sahlab* (see p. 149)
140g sugar
300ml double cream

A few drops of rose
essence (if you are unable to
source it, you can substitute
100ml rose water in this
recipe)
A few drops of red food
colouring

1. Mix together the *sahlab* and the sugar.
2. Add the milk and single cream.
3. Pour the mixture into a heavy-based saucepan and bring to boiling, stirring constantly with a wooden spatula. Add the food colouring and rose essence.
4. Remove from the heat and leave to cool.
5. Once the mixture is cool, pour half into your ice-cream maker and set it going for 30 minutes, or until ice cream has formed. Keep the other half of the mixture cold while the first batch of ice cream is being made. When this batch is ready, scoop your ice cream into a serving bowl and replace with the other half of the mixture, to prepare in the same way.
6. Serve and eat immediately.

COMMENTS

- The *sahlab* most widely available is already sweetened. If you are using pure powdered *sahlab*, you will need to add a further 60g sugar, so 200g sugar in total for this recipe.

Coffee

Traditionally, the coffee beans imported into Lebanon came from
Ceylon, Brazil and also Yemen, whose two port towns, Aden and
especially Mokha, will forever be associated with the history
of coffee. For unsweetened coffee, beans from Aden or Ceylon
were used; for sweetened coffee, Brazilian beans were preferred.
Today, the majority of coffee beans imported into Lebanon are
from Brazil. Until the 1980s, Lebanese-style coffee was known as
"Turkish coffee", a name still sometimes used today. The process for
preparing it has remained unchanged. The beans are roasted until
they begin to exude their oil and turn a very dark brown. Then they
are ground as finely as possible so that they give the richest aroma.
The coffee jug itself is made of stainless steel or brass, and specially
adapted for use on the stove: it has a long handle and the rim is
narrower than the base, in order to limit evaporation.

BLACK COFFEE

SERVES 6

1. Pour 7 coffee-cups of water into the coffee jug. Set on the heat.
2. As soon as the water begins to boil, remove from the heat and add 7 level teaspoons ground coffee. Put the coffee jug back on the heat, allow the coffee to bubble up and once again remove from the heat.
3. When some foam has gathered on the surface, scoop it off with a spoon so that you can allow a little for each cup. Return the jug to the heat and let the coffee bubble up a second time.
4. Serve in small coffee cups. Avoid drinking the grounds that settle at the bottom.

WHITE COFFEE

This kind of "coffee" is a recent invention, unknown in Lebanon before the 1960s. In some families, it was customary to add a few drops of orange-blossom water to each cup of coffee. Someone had the idea of simply adding the drops to hot water. The fashion spread first in Beirut, then through the rest of the country. The new drink, taken with or without sugar, no longer bore any relation to coffee, but the name has remained, due to its origins.

SERVES 6

1. Pour 7 coffee-cups of water into the coffee jug and bring to the boil.
2. Remove from the heat and add one coffee-cup of orange-blossom water (see p. 169), or 1 tablespoon per cup.
3. Serve.

ANISEED KAAK

In the Middle East, kaak *refers to a range of biscuit-like cakes.*

PREPARATION: 15 MINS

COOKING 12–15 MINS

SERVES 6

250g fine white flour

100g butter at room
temperature

75g caster sugar

2 tablespoons aniseed seeds

1 teaspoon raising agent

3 tablespoons milk

1. Pre-heat the oven to 150°C (gas mark 5).
2. Rub the flour into the butter, then add the sugar, aniseed, raising agent and milk, stirring until you have a smooth paste.
3. Shape this into "sausages" of 1.5cm diameter and then cut them into 3cm-long sections. Lay them out on an oven tray lined with greaseproof paper.
4. Bake for 12–15 minutes.

VARIATION

- You can substitute sesame seeds for aniseed if you prefer.

KAAK TETA NAZEERA

The word teta, *usually followed by a first name, is the traditional word for grandmother. Teta Nazeera Maalouf (1895–1986) created this recipe.*

PREPARATION: 15 MINS

COOKING: 12–15 MINS

SERVES 6

400g fine white flour

125g butter at room
temperature

100ml milk

100g caster sugar

1 tablespoon ground
cinnamon

1 sachet or 7.5g vanilla sugar

4 teaspoons raising agent

1. Pre-heat the oven to 150°C (gas mark 5).
2. Combine the flour and butter, then add the raising agent, sugar, cinnamon and vanilla, then the milk, until you have a smooth paste. Shape small "sausages" out of it, of 1cm diameter, then cut them into sections roughly 8cm long. Bring the ends of each together to form into rings, then lay them out on a baking tray lined with greaseproof paper.
3. Bake for 12 to 15 minutes.

COMMENTS

- If you are using a food processor, keep the butter cold until you add it to the flour, in order to avoid the mixture warming up.

SFOUF

PREPARATION: 15 MINS

RESTING FOR THE DOUGH:

1 HR

COOKING: 20 MINS

SERVES 6

300g fine wheat semolina

250g fine white flour

300g caster sugar

400ml whole milk

50g butter at room
temperature

100g vegetable oil

1 teaspoon ground aniseed

1 teaspoon turmeric

1 teaspoon raising agent

25 pine nuts (see p. 163)

1 teaspoon *tahini* (see p. 167)

1. Combine the flour and semolina with the butter and oil. Add the sugar and ground aniseed, the turmeric and the raising agent. Finally, add the milk and mix thoroughly.
2. Coat a tart tin of about 30 cm diameter with *tahini*. On this, spread out the *sfouf* dough, flattening it with wet hands so that the dough does not stick to them.
3. Sprinkle with pine nuts.
4. Set aside for 1 hour. 15 minutes before the end of this period, pre-heat the oven to 250°C (gas mark 8–9).
5. When the hour is over, put the *sfouf* in the oven and bake for 20 minutes.
6. Remove from the oven and leave to cool. Then cut into square or diamond-shaped sections, of about 3cm across.
7. These cakes will keep for a week in a properly sealed container.

VARIATION

- You can substitute carob molasses (see p. 166) for the sugar, if you prefer.

Lebanese Products

BULGUR WHEAT

This form of cooked cracked wheat features heavily in the cookery of Lebanon and its neighbours; we call it *bourghol*. The preparation of bulgur in each village used once to be an occasion for celebration, especially for the children, for whom sweet, wheat-based dishes with dried fruit were cooked. Today, the social side of the occasion has almost faded away, although the preparation technique has remained the same. The wheat is boiled, sun-dried on roof-tops, then crushed in great millstones; it is then sieved, to separate the coarse wheat from the fine and to remove the bran and any impurities.

This technique is thought to come from India where, for centuries, a form of sterilisation has been carried out on rice. In a process similar to that for making bulgur, the grains are sterilised, all flora as well as bacteria are destroyed and the starch is toughened, becoming more resistant without losing its nutritional qualities. Admittedly, the vitamin content is slightly reduced but the proteins in each grain are not affected. Similarly treated, bulgur can be kept much longer than ordinary, untreated wheat.

Fine bulgur, white or brown, is used for dishes such as *kibbeh*. It only needs to be soaked in cold water, then drained, to be rid of the surplus water. For *tabbouleh*, the bulgur can either be soaked and drained as for *kibbeh*, or it can be added as it is, so that it will absorb more of the tomato and lemon juices and remain slightly crunchier.

Coarse bulgur, white or brown, needs to be cooked in water or stock for 15 minutes and may substitute for rice in many recipes. It has the advantage of not sticking to the pan during cooking. On the other hand, even though bulgur superficially resembles couscous, it is not advisable to use the one product in recipes calling for the other. They are quite different products and behave differently on heating as well as in cold dishes.

Apart from the "classic" varieties, there is a form of bulgur wheat, originally from Egypt, called Kamut, which has much larger grains than those of ordinary wheat. Another, made from spelt, can be considered the forefather of modern wheat. This last, brown-coloured bulgur closely resembles that found traditionally in Lebanese villages. It must be soaked for 10 minutes in hot water before cooking, as it is slightly larger and firmer than everyday bulgur. It is widely known as "spelta".

Bulgur can be bought in all Middle-Eastern food shops and in health food shops.

LEBANESE BREADS

While there are many varieties of Lebanese bread, with different traditional backgrounds, its principal characteristic never varies: it must be supple, so it can be broken, or rather torn, then folded into a pocket, in order to scoop up a mouthful of *labneh*, hummus, *moutabal* or some other *mezze*. Lebanese bread is, in a sense, simply another table implement, only an edible one: the *sine qua non* of Lebanese meals.

The most widely available bread is known as *khobz baladi* or *khobz kmej*. This is bread made in cities. It is this bread that is called for in the recipes given here, although commercial pitta bread is a good substitute.

Khobz baladi looks like a risen loaf when taken straight from the oven; however, it is hollow inside and will deflate slowly as it cools. The top and bottom hemispheres flatten down into two circles lying one on top of the other. It is similar to Greek pitta, only larger and thinner, therefore more pliable. We call it *khobz abiad* when it is made with white flour, and *khobz asmar* if wholemeal flour has been used.

Other kinds of bread can be found in the villages. One kind looks like a large round crêpe, about 50cm in diameter, and can be folded like a napkin. This is known as *khobz marqouk*, which means "thinned", or *khobz sage*, after the word for the special hotplate on which it is cooked, a black metal convex circle, about 60cm in diameter. The soft uncooked dough of this bread is very lightly salted, so that it remains elastic. After kneading, it should be stretched out, then spun in the air, passed back and forth from hand to hand, so that it grows even wider and thinner. Next, the bread is set on a round pad, which is used either to lay it on the sage itself or to help it stick to the sides of the oven. The bread cooks very quickly so is peeled off almost immediately and stacked in towers of identical wide, flat breads.

Another, thicker village bread is known as *khobz tannour*, after the oven in which it is baked – indeed its name suggests kinship with the Indian tandoor. In its Lebanese form, this oven consists of a cylinder about 80cm high, built of brick and earth and narrowing slightly towards the top, with an opening near the base to admit wood for fuel. As soon as the flames have died down and the embers are ready, the dough, drawn out into a circle, is laid on a round pad and then in turn stuck to the interior wall of the *tannour* and taken out again after a few seconds.

Tannour bread and *sage* bread are made with the same ingredients as bread in the cities, which are: wheat flour, baker's yeast, salt and water, to which are added barley flour and corn flour. Unfortunately, bakers today often add sugar, to speed up the dough's fermentation and make it stretchier and finer.

Until the 1960s, bread was baked in communal ovens in the villages. Women brought along their dough, shaped their bread on the bakery's great stone table, flattened it and left it on the bakery's long wooden planks; then the baker would bake each family's bread in turn. The bread was thicker than is usual these days, and more irregular. Little by little, industrially baked bread has taken over and these traditions have begun to disappear.

Towards the end of a batch of baking, it was common to bake *tlameh*: little oval buns, sweet or savoury, eaten hot as they came or with other food, such as big *fatayers* stuffed with spinach or purslane, or with a lamb confit called *awarma*, or with *kishk*, a dish made with yoghurt and cracked wheat that is dried and simply re-heated to be eaten.

There is also another kind of bread that we call *khobz jrish*. It is known as *tlameh* in some areas and as *baqaa* in others. This bread is made from brown flour and whole wheat, which is not boiled like bulgur. This cracked wheat is set to soak, then mixed with the flour, some raising agent, salt and sometimes aniseed. When ready to bake, the baker dips his hands in olive oil and shapes the breads, rounded in the South and oval in the Baalbek area. This bread used to be made for special religious and social occasions and distributed to all the villagers.

SUMAC

Sumac comes in the form of an astringent powder, burgundy in colour and with an acidic taste. In Lebanese cookery, it is used like this, or diluted in a little water; conveniently, its flavour is not altered by cooking. Made of berries gathered from the conical bunches of the small *sumac* bush, which grows wild in Mediterranean areas, *sumac* was traditionally used in the tanning of leather. The plant's Latin name, *Rhus coriaria*, recalls this former use. The common local name is *summaq*; the consonants "s", "m" and "q" making up the Aramaic word for "red".

There are many varieties of *sumac* from all round the world, some of them poisonous. In Canada it is known as *vinaigrier*. It is easily distinguishable there in the autumn by its magnificent red leaves.

The bunches of *sumac* are harvested before the rainy season, then dried for 10 to 15 days in the sun. Traditionally, the berries should also be picked off the bunch, so that only they are retained. Usually, the powder is prepared in advance. The dried berries are poured into a thick bag and beaten with a wooden pestle. The resulting powder is then passed through a fine sieve. Only what comes through is edible; the berries that are left are poisonous.

In traditional Lebanese medicine, a small spoonful of *sumac*, diluted in a glass of water, was recommended to calm mild gastric upsets. In Lebanese cookery, it is used in *fattoush* and some other salads, although not in *tabbouleh*. It is also used in marinades; a small spoonful is plenty.

Sumac can be found in Middle-Eastern food shops. You will, however, need to make sure that the product you are given does not contain citric acid – a frequent practice, sadly, and often not noted on packaging. This makes it even more important to choose high-quality products. In any case, you should not buy *sumac* in large quantities; from experience, and to put this in some perspective, a whole family's annual consumption of *sumac* would not normally exceed 500g.

PINE NUTS

Pine nuts adorn the most ordinary dishes and lend them a festive feel. Usually roasted, they are often added to rice, *fatteh* and many other dishes. They are essential for meat-based *kibbeh*. They can even be crushed up with raw *kibbeh* as a substitute for some of the fat.

Pine nuts are actually the seeds of pine cones that take two years to ripen. Harvested from pine trees in the autumn, the cones are first stored away from moisture and covered with branches, to avoid any premature opening. Only in the following June are they brought out and laid on roofs, to stay drying in the sun throughout the summer. Once they have opened, they are put into large sacks and beaten, so that the pine "nuts" come away from the cones. The nuts are then washed in a basin of water, which makes their husks tougher so they can be hulled without damaging the kernel inside.

ZAATAR

A product that is symbolic of Lebanon and the surrounding countries, *zaatar* is an aromatic plant with a taste similar to thyme, oregano or summer savory. The word *zaatar* also designates the different mixtures of herbs and spices in which *zaatar* is the dominant flavour. Its Latin name is *Origanum orientalis*.

Zaatar grows wild in arid regions. It is harvested in summer when it blossoms. It is dried, the leaves stripped from the stems and packed into canvas bags, then beaten to a powder inside the bags. This is then sifted and all twigs removed. The flowers are the most prized element, for they have the most concentrated flavour as well as the medicinal properties.

Zaatar can be eaten as it is in salads, with or without onions, sometimes with tomatoes, seasoned with oil and lemon juice or vinegar. Nevertheless it is most commonly eaten dry, mixed with other condiments or seasonings.

Zaatar mixtures vary according to region and personal tastes. Apart from the *zaatar* itself, the basic ingredients are *sumac*, roasted sesame seeds and salt. But it is also common to find spices such as cumin or aniseed mixed in. In the Syrian city of Aleppo, traditionally one of the centres of Middle-Eastern cuisine, *zaatar* is often made with the addition of ground pistachios.

In the 19th century, Henry Guys, a French consul who had been posted to Saïda (now in southern Lebanon), published a description of the landscape and mores in which he gently poked fun at the local people, so partial to *zaatar* that they would eat it all day long. If they had to travel far from home, they would pay exorbitant prices to make sure they had enough for the journey, so incapable were they of doing without it. In fact, *zaatar* is eaten at any time of day, but above all at breakfast: mixed into olive oil, it goes with *labneh*, the drained and salted yoghurt which is another key element of Lebanese food. It is also often eaten at tea-time; even today street vendors wander the streets at the end of the afternoon calling out: "'Asriyé!". '*Asriyé' kaak* is a hard, rounded wheaten bread that is covered with sesame seeds, golden and crusty and stuffed with *zaatar*. Its name comes from '*asr*, which refers to the setting sun – as represented by the off-centre fist-sized hole that seems to be forever "sinking" towards the edge of this special bread. This is the snack traditionally eaten by children on their way home from school.

Zaatar can be bought already mixed in Middle-Eastern food shops, but you can also make your own mixture. Connoisseurs of *zaatar* may prefer to bring their favourite mixture directly from their own village. Thus, they hope to ensure their product is of the highest quality, uncontaminated with the wrong herbs and with the maximum proportion of *zaatar* flowers. There are often no flowers at all in the commercial versions; the gathering of *zaatar* being unregulated, pickers rush to hit their quotas ahead of others without even waiting for the plants to flower.

SPICES

While Lebanese cookery calls for many different spices, the aim is to multiply flavours, not to accentuate any peppery heat. The food can hardly be called "spicy" for it will never 'take the roof off' your palate or tongue. Even the allspice used in a range of recipes is mild, subtle and scented. This is a variety of spice similar to a peppercorn and also known as Jamaican pepper; the peppercorns are about the size of petits pois and their flavour evokes that of cinnamon, cloves and nutmeg.

We also use several spice mixes of varying composition.

THE ALEPPO MIX OR 5 SPICE MIX

100g mild white pepper
25g black pepper
25g nutmeg
17g cloves
7g green cardamom powder

Ideally, you will have access to a spice-mill at home and so will be able to grind small quantities of spices as you need them. They keep better whole than ready-ground.

THE 7 SPICE MIX

For this mix, grind together the following ingredients:
½ a nutmeg
1 tablespoon black pepper
1 tablespoon coriander seeds
1 tablespoon cumin seeds
1 tablespoon cloves
1 stick cinnamon
Seeds of 10 whole green cardamoms

DEBS REMMANE

POMEGRANATE MOLASSES

This is the concentrated juice of sour pomegranates – a bright red syrup. Each fruit is carefully de-seeded and the bitter yellow skins that divide each section are removed. The juice is collected, purified by sieving and boiled until it becomes thick. A little salt is added at the end of the process. Roughly 7 to 10 litres of sour pomegranate juice is required to make just one litre of *debs remmane*. The molasses tastes sharp but also slightly sweet. This product can easily be found in Middle-Eastern food shops, but you need to make sure you are sold true *debs remmane*, made in the traditional way, and not a syrup of citric acid that has merely been coloured with caramel.

CAROB MOLASSES

Carob trees grow naturally in many Lebanese villages. The pods start off green and are very astringent at this stage; the green pods used to be used to curdle milk for homemade cheese. When they mature, in September, the pods turn black. At this point they are picked, crushed in a press, then sifted and preserved in glass jars.

Known as *debs kharroub*, this molasses has the consistency of honey. It can be prepared by pouring a little into a bowl, adding a few spoonfuls of *tahini* and mixing these together. This makes a thick, sticky liquid, which is eaten with pieces of bread.

Carob molasses sometimes also appears in health-food products, as a sugar substitute.

GRAPE MOLASSES

This molasses should be made from a variety of grape similar to the common wine-grape "chasselas". It is a juicy, thin-skinned grape. Once ripe, the bunches are picked, mouldy grapes discarded and the remainder pressed then filtered through fine muslin. The resulting juice is then boiled and reduced to a third of its original volume. Next it is beaten for several minutes with a large wooden spoon, until it becomes like thick, opaque honey, so that it doesn't crystallise. Known as *debs enab*, this molasses is eaten all year round.

In the villages, there used to be a fad for a very simple dessert made from grape molasses and called *harrouq osboh*, which means "finger-burner". Lebanese bread was cut into strips and fried until golden in a pan, a few spoonfuls of grape molasses were then poured over it and it was eaten just like that, very hot, the children doing their best to avoid burning their fingers.

Another memory from our childhood is of *yaasama*, which can only be made in snowy areas in the winter. We used to gather fine virgin snow in glasses, then pour a good glassful of grape molasses over it and savour an icy dessert.

TAHINI

SESAME PASTE

Sesame is ubiquitous in Lebanese cuisine, as indeed it is in many other Middle-Eastern countries. It seems to have been discovered long ago, being mentioned in Mesopotamian stone tablets as the 'oil plant'. For centuries, a range of nutritional and gastronomic properties has been attributed to it. Modern science has found sesame to have high levels of phosphorus and lecithin, substances reputed to be good for the brain. It is doubtless due to this tiny seed's impressive aroma when crushed, its panoply of benefits and its versatility, that the mysterious, anonymous authors of the *Thousand and One Nights* came up with the magic formula "Open, Sesame!"

Sesame seeds can be eaten whole, in oil form or as a paste – in Lebanon the paste is called *tahini*. According to the traditional method, the raw sesame seeds are crushed in a stone mill, which prevents their over-heating. Oil is extracted from the resulting mixture, a separate product from the paste that remains, which becomes *tahini*. Sesame oil is a good frying oil, since it does not burn easily. Take care not to confuse it with the roasted sesame oil used in Asian cooking, which has a much more pronounced taste.

Sesame paste, or *tahini*, is an important element in a number of Lebanese foods such as hummus or aubergine *moutabal*. Combined with lemon juice, it turns into an unctuous sauce called *tarator*, which always accompanies fish dishes. When hot, Lebanese call this *tajine*, because it is the basis for the fish *tajine* dish. It is also served with fish *kibbeh*.

Like many other products made from sesame, *tahini* is widely available.

FREEKEH

Freekeh is little known outside the Middle East, even though this preparation of crunchy roasted wheat is mentioned several times in the Bible. It is thought that an accidental fire was behind the invention of *freekeh*.

For successful *freekeh*, it is essential that the wheat be harvested while it is still green. If harvested too early, the seeds will disintegrate; if harvested too late, they will have lost their green colour and softness. Choosing the correct moment is a delicate decision: when it is the right time, a white milky liquid should appear when the grains of wheat are pinched between two fingers. After gathering, the sheaves of wheat are dried in the sun for two hours. Then they are mixed with barley straw and burnt to the ground, shaken up occasionally with a fork to ensure that the flames have reached every part. They are then left to cool for several hours, after which the ears are threshed to shake out the grain. This is then left to dry in the shade, so that it will not be bleached by the sun.

When fresh, *freekeh* can be eaten uncooked; its taste is subtle and unusual, at once sweet and smoky. In Europe, it is most commonly available in dried form in Middle-Eastern food shops.

MAZAHR

ORANGE-BLOSSOM WATER

Seville orange blossoms, which we call *bousfeir* in Lebanon, are picked in the spring to make *mazahr*, which literally means "flower water". All green parts are stripped away from the petals, which are then combined with twice their volume of water in the tank of a still. This is set on a fierce heat, which is then turned down to a low flame for the rest of the distillation. The steam rising from the water carries the flavour and essence of the blossoms; this follows all the twists of the still's tubes, cools down and condenses and finally falls in drops of orange-blossom water into a vessel at the end of the system. This liquid is then bottled. Neroli, a yellow essential oil, comes to the surface – its presence is the sign of true *mazahr*.

MAWARD

ROSE WATER

In Lebanon, a particular variety of rose called *ward jouri* is distilled to make rose water. Sometimes other rose varieties are used, notably Ispahan or Damask. The flowers are picked at dawn, before the sun can spoil their scent. The petals are removed and placed in a basin of water, with about 1kg of petals to 2 litres of water. This mixture is poured into the still and set on a low flame to avoid burning the fragile petals. Similar plant varieties are used for rose jam and jelly, only their petals are thicker and withstand heat better.

WHERE TO FIND LEBANESE PRODUCTS AND SPICES

If you can't find a specialist Middle-Eastern shop near you, don't hesitate to ask for recommendations from a Lebanese restaurant.

MIDDLE EASTERN SPECIALTY SHOPS

IN LONDON

Al Mustafa
133 Edgware Road, London W2 2HR
Tel. 020 7402 7707

Damas Gate
81-85 Uxbridge Road, London W12 8NR
Tel. 020 8743 5116

Green Valley
37 Upper Berkeley Street, London W1H 5QE
Tel. 020 7402 7385

Le Comptoir Libanais
65 Wigmore Street, London W1U 1PZ
Tel. 020 7935 1110

Lebanese Food Centre
153 The Vale , London, W3 7RH
Tel. 020 8740 7365

Maroush Deli
45-49 Edgware Road, London W2 2HZ
Tel. 020 7723 3666

Noura
12 William Street, London SW1X 9HL
Tel. 020 7235 5900

Phoenicia
186-188 Kentish Town Road, London NW5
Tel. 020 7267 1267

Zen
27 Moscow Road, London W2 4AH
Tel. 020 7792 2058

IN MANCHESTER

Al Faisal
2-4 Slade Lane, Manchester M13 0QE
Tel. 01 61 251 3392

Farooq Food Store
169 Dickenson Road, Manchester M13 0YN
Tel. 01 61 224 1158

Venus Foods
45 Anson Road, Manchester M14 5DE
Tel. 01 61 256 1110

Worldwide Food Store
401 Great Western Street, Manchester M14 4AH
Tel. 01 61 248 6727

IN BRIGHTON

Taj Mahal International Foods
95 Western Road, Brighton BN1 2 AD
Tel. 01 273 325027

IN GLASGOW

Scherezade
47 Bank Street, Hillhead, Glasgow G12 8NE
Tel. 0141 334 2121

WEBSITES

buylebanese.com
mymoune.com
aldoukan.com

Acknowledgements

I would never have undertaken this book without the persistent encouragement of my husband, Amin, my sons Ruchdi, Tarek and Ziad, and also that of Richard Ducousset and Danièle Boespflug.

Embarked on the adventure, I would never have been able to complete it without Karim Haïdar's precious friendship, without Laure Paoli's and Myrtille Chareyre's generous advice, without the skills of Sabine Paris, Caroline Faccioli and Frédéric Agid, and those of Lulu Norman and Sophie Lewis in this elegant English translation.

Throughout the last two years I've also had the benefit of endless advice from my friends and my vast family. Since I cannot name everyone I wish to thank here, I will only mention those whose contribution has been most effective and most constant: Ghada Maamari, Jacqueline Jraissaty, Nelly Maamari, Sylvie Tabet, Marlène Nasr, Hind Maalouf, Leyla Zoghbi, Nada Maalouf Labbé, Dolly Sofia, Mymouné as represented by Leyla Maalouf and Youmna Ghorayeb, Liza Soughayar and Liza restaurant, Eliane Kreiker, Claire Bassoul, Mona Touzani, Mary Salamé and Yolla Féghali Saliba.

Andrée Maalouf

Thank you, Mum, for your affection and your help throughout my adventures as a cook,
Thank you, Dad, for always believing in me,
Thank you, Aunt Mona, for teaching me my first Lebanese dishes,
Thank you, Teta, my grandmother, for passing on the gene for a passion for cooking.

Thank you Andrée, Amin, Sabine, Caroline, Frédéric, Myrtille and Laure, who made this book with me.

Thank you to Salim and Rabih from Sorbet&Co for their vital help concerning ice cream

Warmest thanks to the young team at La Branche d'Olivier, Lebanese seafood restaurant (44, rue de Naples, 75008 Paris. Tel: (00 33) 1 45 63 28 92) www.labranchedolivier.fr

Karim Haïdar

The translators, Lulu Norman and Sophie Lewis, would especially like to thank Andrée Maalouf and Karim Haïdar, and also Caroline Conran, Tarfa Salam and Jeremy Lee, for their unflagging help in the translation process.

INDEX

INDEX OF RECIPES BY PRINCIPAL INGREDIENTS

RECIPES FOLLOWED BY (V) ARE VARIATIONS

Almond
    Five spice lamb and rice 102
    Ksheif, rose-scented salad of dried
    apricots and nuts 137
    Leg of lamb and rice with broad
    beans 101
    Maqloubet-batenjan, aubergine
    layer cake 108
    Meghli 131
    Seven spice chicken and rice 107
    Snayniyeh 138
   Ground
    Walnut marzipan cake 130

Aniseed
    Aniseed ka'ak 155
   Ground
    Maakaroun 144
    Sfouf 156

Apple
    Apples and bananas with
    cinnamon 145

Apricot, dried
    Ksheif, rose-scented salad of dried
    apricots and nuts 137

Arak
    Pears in arak 142

Artichoke heart
    Artichoke hearts and broad bean
    salad 18
    Yakhnet-ardichawkeh, artichoke
    heart ragout 73

Asparagus, green
    Fattet-halioun, with asparagus 80

Aubergine
    Aubergine fatteh 79
    Aubergine maghmour 24
    Aubergine with ewe's milk
    yoghurt 83
    Maqloubet-batenjan, aubergine
    layer cake 108
    Masbaht-al-darwish 112
    Moutabal 27
    Royal sea bream with
    aubergine 118
    Sheikh al-mehshi, stuffed
    aubergines 88

    The Sultan of fish, with deep-fried
    cauliflower and aubergine 123

Banana
    Apples and bananas with
    cinnamon 145

Beans
   Green
    Fattet-khodra, with vegetables 82
    Masbaht-al-darwish 112
    Winter vegetable soup 56
   Haricot
    Yakhnet-fassouliah, white bean
    ragout 78
   Runner
    Green beans with olive oil 22
    Yakhnet-loubieh, green bean
    ragout 77

Beef (minced)
    Fried kibbeh balls 63
    Hamiss, sweet onion soup 55
    Kaftah nayyeh, tartare of kaftah 94
    Kibbeh bil-saynieh, oven-baked
    kibbeh 68
    Kibbeh meshwiyeh 64
    Kibbeh nayyeh, tartare of kibbeh 65
    Kibbeh with yoghurt 69

Beetroot
    Kibbeh meshwiyeh 64

Bread
    Aubergine fatteh 79
    Fattet-halioun, with asparagus 80
    Fattet-hummus, with chickpeas 80
    Fattet-khodra, with vegetables 82
    Fattoush 15
    Royal mouloukhieh 106
    The Sultan of fish, with deep-fried
    cauliflower and aubergine 123

Broad beans
    Artichoke hearts and broad bean
    salad 18
    Leg of lamb and rice with broad
    beans 101
   Dried
    Falafel 36

Bulgur wheat
    Bulgur bedfeen 104

    Bulgur wheat with tomato 111
    Fish balls with coriander (v) 66
    Fish kibbeh 66
    Fried kibbeh balls 63
    Hamiss, sweet onion soup 55
    Kibbeh bil-saynieh, oven-baked
    kibbeh 68
    Kibbeh meshwiyeh 64
    Kibbeh nayyeh, tartare of kibbeh 65
    Kibbeh with yoghurt 69
    Potato kibbeh 60
    Pumpkin kibbeh 62
    Tabbouleh 16

Cabbage
    Stuffed cabbage leaves 88

Caraway
    Bulgur bedfeen 104
    Meghli 131
    Sayadieh 116

Cardamom
    Aleppo mix or 5 spice mix 165
    Five spice lamb and rice 102
    Seven spice mix 165

Carob molasses
    Pears in arak 142

Carrot
    Aubergine maghmour 24
    Fattet-khodra, with vegetables 82
    Fish freekeh 124
    Five spice lamb and rice 102
    Freekket-touyour
    with three birds 104
    Masbaht-al-darwish 112
    Winter vegetable soup 56
    Yakhnet-bazella, pea ragout 74
    Yellow lentil soup 54

Cauliflower
    The Sultan of fish, with deep-fried
    cauliflower and aubergine 123

Celery
    Fattet-khodra, with vegetables 82
    Stuffed cabbage leaves 88
    Winter vegetable soup 56

Chicken
    Chicken hrisseh (v) 110

Chicken soup with vermicelli 55
Royal mouloukhieh 106
Seven spice chicken and rice 107
Shish taouk 98

Chickpeas
Aubergine maghmour 24
Bulgur bedfeen 104
Falafel 36
Fattet-hummus, with chickpeas 80
Hummus 30

Cinnamon
Ground
Apples and bananas with
cinnamon 145
Bulgur bedfeen 104
Falafel 36
Five spice lamb and rice 102
Ka'ak Teta Nazira 155
Meghli 131
Sticks
Chicken hrisseh (v) 110
Lamb and wheat hrisseh with
cinnamon 110
Seven spice mix 165

Coconut, grated
Meghli 131

Cod
Fish balls with coriander (v) 66
Fish kibbeh 66

Coriander
Adas bi hamod, lentil soup with
Swiss chard and lemon 52
Coral lentil soup with
tomato 54
Falafel 36
Fish balls with coriander (v) 66
Fish kibbeh 66
Kibbeh with yoghurt 69
Octopus salad with coriander 119
Potato kibbeh 60
Royal mouloukhieh 106
Spicy grey mullet 118
Squid with garlic and coriander 120
Yakhnet-batata, potato ragout 76
Yakhnet-bazella, pea ragout 74
Yakhnet-bemieh, Greek horn or
okra ragout 72
Yakhnet-fassouliah, white bean
ragout 78
Yakhnet-loubieh, green bean
ragout 77
Seeds
Seven spice mix 165

Courgette
Ablama, selection of stuffed
vegetables 86
Courgettes moutabal 28
Falafel 36
Fattet-khodra, with
vegetables 82
Koussa bil-laban, courgettes
stuffed with lamb and yoghurt 84
Masbaht-al-darwish 112
Stuffed courgettes and stuffed
vine leaves 89
Winter vegetable soup 56

Cucumber
Fattoush 15
Khiar bi laban, yoghurt with
cucumber 69

Cumin
Seven spice mix 165
Ground
Adas bi hamod, lentil soup with
Swiss chard and lemon 52
Five spice lamb and rice 102
Sayadieh 116
Spicy grey mullet 118
Tomatoes with cumin 18

Currants
Ksheif, rose-scented salad of dried
apricots and nuts 137

Cuttlefish
Sabbidij, cuttlefish in ink 122

Date
Easter maamoul 134

Dill
Fish kaftah (v) 94

Fish stock
Fish freekeh 124
Sayadieh 116

Freekeh
Fish freekeh 124
Freekket-touyour with three
birds 104

Gum Arabic
Rose ice cream 151
Sahlab ice cream 151
Strawberry ice cream 150

Halloumi cheese
Fried halloumi 48

Rekakats, pastry wraps with
cheese and parsley 40

Halva
Halva ice cream 150

Labneh
Labneh 49
Shanklish in salad 47

Lamb
Cutlets
Lamb cutlets with 7 spices 97
Fat
Kibbeh meshwiyeh 64
Leg
Leg of lamb and rice with broad
beans 101
Minced
Ablama, selection of stuffed
vegetables 86
Aubergine fatteh 79
Aubergine with ewe's milk
yoghurt 83
Bulgur wheat with tomato 111
Daoud basha, minced lamb
balls 111
Fried kaftah meatballs 95
Fried kibbeh balls 63
Hamiss, sweet onion soup 55
Kaftah nayyeh, tartare of kaftah 94
Kibbeh bil-saynieh, oven-baked
kibbeh 68
Kibbeh meshwiyeh 64
Kibbeh nayyeh, tartare of
kibbeh 65
Kibbeh with yoghurt 69
Koussa bil-laban, stuffed cour-
gettes with lamb and yoghurt 84
Lahm bi ajeen, tartlets with lamb
and tomatoes 42
Maqloubet-batenjan, aubergine
layer cake 108
Oven-baked kaftah 93
Sambousiks 41
Seven spice chicken and rice 107
Stuffed cabbage leaves 88
Stuffed courgettes and stuffed
vine leaves 89
Yellow lentil soup 54
Rib
Stuffed courgettes and stuffed
vine leaves 89
Saddle
Leg of lamb and rice with broad
beans 101
Shank
Bulgur bedfeen 104
Lamb and wheat hrisseh with

cinnamon 110
Winter vegetable soup 56
Shoulder
Five spice lamb and rice 102
Grilled kaftah 94
Masbaht-al-darwish 112
Winter vegetable soup 56
Yakhnet-ardichawkeh, artichoke
heart ragout 73
Yakhnet-batata, potato ragout 76
Yakhnet-bazella, pea ragout 74
Yakhnet-bemieh, okra ragout 72
Yakhnet-fassouliah, white bean
ragout 78
Yakhnet-loubieh, green bean
ragout 77

Lentils
Coral
Coral lentil moujaddara 35
Coral lentil soup with tomato 54
Green
Moujaddara, a biblical dish 34
Red
Moujaddara, a biblical dish 34
Yellow
Adas bi hamod, lentil soup with
Swiss chard and lemon 52
Moudardara, yellow lentil salad 33
Yellow lentil soup 54

Mahlab
Easter maamoul 134
Maakaroun 144

Mascarpone
Atayef-bil-ashta 132
Osmallieh 146

Mastic
Haytalieh 128
Sahlab ice cream 151

Mint
Falafel 36
Fattoush 15
Kibbeh nayyeh, tartare of
kibbeh 65
Stuffed cabbage leaves 88
Stuffed vine leaves 21
Tabbouleh 16
Dried
Khiar bi laban, yoghurt with
cucumber 69
Kibbeh meshwiyeh 64
Koussa bil-laban, stuffed cour-
gettes with lamb and yoghurt 84
Pumpkin kibbeh 62
Stuffed cabbage leaves 88

Monkfish
Fish balls with coriander (v) 66
Fish kibbeh 66

Mouloukhieh
Royal mouloukhieh 106

Mozzarella
Atayef-bil-ashta 132
Osmallieh 146

Mullet, grey
Spicy grey mullet 118

Mullet, red
Fish freekeh 124

Nutmeg
Aleppo mix or 5 spice mix 165
Seven spice mix 165

Octopus
Octopus salad with coriander 119

Okra
Okra with olive oile, bemieh bzeit
22
Yakhnet-bemieh, okra ragout 72

Olives, black
Rocket with olives 19

Orange
Bitter
Tajine sauce 29
Juice
Haytalieh 128
Strawberry and orange-blossom
salad 140
Zest
Haytalieh 128

Orange-blossom water
Atayef-bil-ashta 132
Awamats, doughnuts in syrup 136
Easter maamoul 134
Haytalieh 128
Ksheif, rose-scented salad of dried
apricots and nuts 137
Maakaroun 144
Osmallieh 146
Riz-bi-halib, Lebanese rice pud-
ding 145
Sahlab ice cream 151
Snayniyeh 138
Strawberry and orange-blossom
salad 140
Walnut marzipan cake 130

White coffee 154

Partridge
Freekket-touyour with three birds
104

Pastry sheets
Brick
Rekakats, pastry wraps with
cheese and parsley 40
Filo
Rekakats, pastry wraps with
cheese and parsley 40

Pastry, vermicelli
Osmallieh 146

Pear
Pears in arak 142

Peas
Fattet-khodra, with vegetables 82
Seven spice chicken and rice 107
Winter vegetable soup 56
Yakhnet-bazella, pea ragout 74

Pepper
Black
Aleppo mix or 5 spice mix 165
Five spice lamb and rice 102
Seven spice chicken and rice 107
Seven spice mix 165
White
Aleppo mix or 5 spice mix 165
Chicken hrisseh (v) 110
Lamb and wheat hrisseh with
cinnamon 110

Pepper, red
Maqloubet-batenjan, aubergine
layer cake 108
Masbaht-al-darwish 112
Oven-baked kaftah 93

Pigeon
Freekket-touyour with three birds
104

Pine nuts
Ablama, selection of stuffed
vegetables 86
Aubergine fatteh 79
Aubergine with ewe's milk
yoghurt 83
Bulgur wheat with tomato 111
Courgettes moutabal 28
Fattet-halioun, with asparagus 80
Fattet-hummus, with chickpeas 80

Fattet-khodra, with vegetables 82
Fish balls with coriander (v) 66
Fish kibbeh 66
Five spice lamb and rice 102
Fried kibbeh balls 63
Hamiss, sweet onion soup 55
Kibbeh bil-saynieh, oven-baked
kibbeh 68
Kibbeh nayyeh, tartare of
kibbeh 65
Kibbeh with yoghurt 69
Ksheif, rose-scented salad of dried
apricots and nuts 137
Leg of lamb and rice with broad
beans 101
Maqloubet-batenjan, aubergine
layer cake 108
Meghli 131
Sambousiks 41
Sayadieh 116
Seven spice chicken and rice 107
Sfouf 156
Snayniyeh 138
Spinach fatayers 44
Stuffed cabbage leaves 88
Swiss chard fatayers (v) 44

Pistachio
Atayef-bil-ashta 132
Easter maamoul 134
Five spice lamb and rice 102
Ksheif, rose-scented salad of dried
apricots and nuts 137
Leg of lamb and rice with broad
beans 101
Maqloubet-batenjan, aubergine
layer cake 108
Meghli 131
Osmallieh 146
Quail with sumac 97
Seven spice chicken and rice 107
Snayniyeh 138

Pollock
Fish balls with coriander (v) 66
Fish kibbeh 66

Pomegranate
Snayniyeh 138
Molasses, debs remmane
Hamiss, sweet onion soup 55
Lahm bi ajeen, tartlets with lamb
and tomatoes 42
Masbaht-al-darwish 112
Oven-baked kaftah 93
Pumpkin kibbeh 62
Royal sea bream with
aubergine 118

Potato
Ablama, selection of stuffed
vegetables 86
Adas bi hamod, lentil soup with
Swiss chard and lemon 52
Fattet-khodra, with vegetables 82
Masbaht-al-darwish 112
Oven-baked kaftah 93
Potato kibbeh 60
Pumpkin kibbeh 62
Stuffed vine leaves 21
Winter vegetable soup 56
Yakhnet-ardichawkeh, artichoke
heart ragout 73
Yakhnet-batata, potato ragout 76
Yellow lentil soup 54

Poussin
Farrouj meshwi, grilled chicken
with garlic 99

Prawns
Fish freekeh 124

Prune
Ksheif, rose-scented salad of dried
apricots and nuts 137

Pumpkin
Pumpkin kibbeh 62

Quail
Freekket-touyour with three
birds 104
Quail with sumac 97

Radish
Falafel 36
Fattoush 15

Raisins
Five spice lamb and rice 102

Rice
Royal mouloukhieh 106
Basmati
Basmati rice 77
Five spice lamb and rice 102
Leg of lamb and rice with broad
beans 101
Maqloubet-batenjan, aubergine
layer cake 108
Moudardara, yellow lentil salad 33
Royal mouloukhieh 106
Royal sea bream with aubergine 118
Sayadieh 116
Seven spice chicken and rice 107
Long grain
Rice with vermicelli 77

Short grain
Coral lentil moujaddara 35
Kibbeh with yoghurt 69
Koussa bil-laban, stuffed cour-
gettes with lamb and yoghurt 84
Moujaddara, a biblical dish 34
Riz-bi-halib, Lebanese rice
pudding 145
Stuffed cabbage leaves 88
Stuffed courgettes and stuffed
vine leaves 89
Stuffed vine leaves 21

Rose water
Easter maamoul 134
Ksheif, rose-scented salad of dried
apricots and nuts 137
Osmallieh 146
Walnut marzipan cake 130
Rose essence
Rose ice cream 151

Saffron
Fish kibbeh 66

Sahlab
Rose ice cream 151
Sahlab ice cream 151
Strawberry ice cream 150

Salad leaves
Rocket
Rocket with olives 19
Romaine lettuce
Fattoush 15
Sucrine lettuce
Fattoush 15

Sea bass
Fish freekeh 124
Sayadieh 116

Sea bream
Fish kaftah (v) 94
Royal sea bream with aubergine
118

Semolina
Easter maamoul 134
Meghli 131
Sfouf 156

Sesame
Seeds
Fried halloumi 48
Tahini
Aubergine fatteh 79
Courgettes moutabal 28
Fattet-hummus, with chickpeas 80

Fattet-khodra, with vegetables 82
Hummus 30
Moutabal 27
Sfouf 156
Swiss chard moutabal 28
Tajine sauce 29
Tarator sauce 29

Seven Spice Mix
Bulgur wheat with tomato 111
Courgettes moutabal 28
Farrouj meshwi, grilled chicken
with garlic 99
Lamb cutlets with 7 spices 97
Leg of lamb and rice with broad
beans 101
Seven spice chicken and rice 107
Shish taouk, chicken kebabs
marinated in 7 spices 98

Spinach
Fatayers with spinach 44

Squid
Squid with garlic and coriander
120

Strawberry
Strawberry and orange-blossom
salad 140

Sultanas
Ksheif, rose-scented salad of dried
apricots and nuts 137

Sumac
Fattoush 15
Kibbeh meshwiyeh 64
Kibbeh nayyeh, tartare of kibbeh
65
Quail with sumac 97
Spinach fatayers 44
Swiss chard fatayers (v) 44

Swiss chard
Adas bi hamod, lentil soup with
Swiss chard and lemon 52
Swiss chard fatayers (v) 44
Swiss chard moutabal 28

Tahini
Aubergine fatteh 79
Courgettes moutabal 28
Fattet-hummus, with chickpeas 80
Fattet-khodra, with vegetables 82
Hummus 30
Moutabal 27
Sfouf 156
Swiss chard moutabal 28

Tajine sauce 29
Tarator sauce 29

Tomato
Ablama, selection of stuffed
vegetables 86
Aubergine fatteh 79
Aubergine maghmour 24
Falafel 36
Fattet-khodra, with vegetables 82
Green beans with olive oil 22
Lahm bi ajeen, tartlets with lamb
and tomatoes 42
Masbaht-al-darwish 112
Octopus salad with coriander 119
Okra with olive oil, bemieh
bzeit 22
Oven-baked kaftah 93
Stuffed cabbage leaves 88
Stuffed vine leaves 21
Tabbouleh 16
Tomatoes with cumin 18
Winter vegetable soup 56
Yakhnet-batata, potato ragout 76
Yakhnet-bazella, pea ragout 74
Yakhnet-bemieh, okra ragout 72
Yakhnet-loubieh, green bean
ragout 77
Cherry
Falafel 36
Fattoush 15
Kibbeh nayyeh, tartare of kibbeh
65
Shanklish in salad 47
Juice
Bulgur wheat with tomato 111
Coral lentil soup with tomato 54
Five spice lamb and rice 102
Oven-baked kaftah 93
Yakhnet-bazella, pea ragout 74
Yakhnet-fassouliah, white bean
ragout 78
Yakhnet-loubieh, green bean
ragout 77

Turmeric
Sfouf 156

Turnip
Falafel 36
Pickled turnips 37

Vermicelli
Chicken soup with vermicelli 55
Rice with vermicelli 77

Vine leaves
Stuffed courgettes and stuffed
vine leaves 89

Stuffed vine leaves 21

Walnut
Easter maamoul 134
Kibbeh meshwiyeh 64
Pumpkin kibbeh 62
Walnut marzipan cake 130

Wheat, hulled
Chicken hrisseh (v) 110
Lamb and wheat hrisseh with
cinnamon 110
Snayniyeh 138

Yoghurt
Ablama, selection of stuffed
vegetables 86
Aubergine fatteh 79
Bulgur bedfeen 104
Fattet-halioun, with asparagus 80
Fattet-hummus, with chickpeas 80
Fattet-khodra, with vegetables 82
Khiar bi laban, yoghurt with
cucumber 69
Kibbeh meshwiyeh 64
Kibbeh with yoghurt 69
Koussa bil-laban, stuffed cour-
gettes with lamb and yoghurt 84
Labneh 49
Lahm bi ajeen, tartlets with lamb
and tomatoes 42
Potato kibbeh 60
Pumpkin kibbeh 62
Sambousiks 41
Ewe's milk
Aubergine with ewe's milk
yoghurt 83
Awamats, doughnuts in syrup 136

Zaatar
Mana'ish, round flat bread with
zaatar 39
Shanklish in salad 47